Voices of F...
in the
Midst
of the
Storm

Reflections of
South Louisiana ELCA Faith Leaders
in the Aftermath
of Hurricane Katrina

Edited by
John McCullough Bade

All proceeds from the sale of this book will go to assist in the Katrina disaster long-term recovery ministries.

Voices of Faith in the Midst of the Storm
Reflections of South Louisiana ELCA Faith Leaders in the Aftermath of Hurricane Katrina

ISBN: 1-4276-0472-X

The cover photo is of Grace Lutheran Church, New Orleans.

The satellite photo on the back cover is from NASA/MODIS, courtesy BBS News, Katrina Collection. Used with permission.

For additional copies of this book, go to:
www.futurewithhopepress.org

For more information on the recovery efforts, log on to:
www.futurewithhope.org

Printed by Lipps Printing, Kenner, LA 70082

Future With Hope Press
Baton Rouge, LA 70808

Contributing Writers

John McCullough Bade – Baton Rouge, LA
Pastor, Writer, Contributing Editor

Sandra Barnes – Slidell, LA
Associate in Ministry
Christ the King Lutheran Church, Kenner, LA

Walton Ehrhardt – Mandeville, LA
Pastoral Counselor, Assistant to the Bishop,
Texas/Louisiana Gulf Coast Synod, ELCA

Bob Hildebrandt – Metairie, LA
Pastor, Retired

Anton Kern – Mandeville, LA
Pastor, Hosanna Lutheran Church, Mandeville, LA

Scott Landrum – New Orleans, LA (West Bank)
Pastor, Love Lutheran Church, New Orleans, LA

Robin McCullough-Bade – Baton Rouge, LA
Interim Pastor, Lutheran Church of Our Saviour,
Baton Rouge, LA

Robert Moore – Houston, TX
Assistant to the Bishop, TX/LA Gulf Coast Synod, ELCA

Jim Shears – Chalmette, LA
Pastor, Gethsemane Lutheran Church, Chalmette, LA

Ron Unger – Kenner, LA
Pastor, Christ the King Lutheran Church, Kenner, LA

Amy Ziettlow – Baton Rouge, LA
Pastor, Hospice of Baton Rouge, LA

Table of Contents

Chapter 4 – Restoration   Pages 61-96

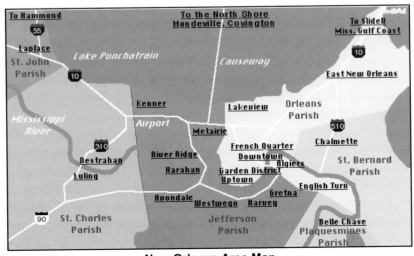

New Orleans Area Map

Introduction

"One Day ... One Word"   **John McCullough Bade**

August 29, 2005 .... Katrina.

Individuals, families, societies, countries, and communities of faith – all have seminal events in their corporate history that shape who they are and who they are to become. Other events become measured in relationship to these significant events. Corporate identity, culture, the ordering of life itself come to be formed and defined by them.

Some events are so intense, so life-changing, so sweeping in their scope and nature that they are known by a single word or a specific date – Pearl Harbor, Hiroshima, Challenger, 9/11.

August 29, 2005 .... Katrina.

For the residents of southeast Louisiana, one day and one word has forever changed life as it was known. The patterns of life, the shaping of civic communities, homes, economies, politics, and communities of faith have been forever changed by Katrina and its aftermath. Even time itself is defined in relationship to the hurricane. "Pre- or post-Katrina?" is now a benchmark to define everything else that occurs.

A Storm of Biblical Proportions

In the reporting of the devastation and destruction of Katrina, the media were often heard saying, "This was a storm of biblical proportions." I'm not sure exactly what was meant by that phrase. Was it to mean that Katrina was on the magnitude of the great flood in Genesis which destroyed everything in its raging water? Was it an allusion to the biblical prophecies of destruction, or to the primordial pre-creation chaotic waters? Or was it perhaps a subtle acknowledgment that humanity is not ultimately in charge?

Perhaps. But I would suggest a different meaning. The people of Israel were shaped by significant, life-changing events – the exodus from Egypt, the passing through the waters of the Red Sea, the destruction of the Temple and the exile into Babylonia, the return and restoration of a city and a way of life. Their culture, mores, and faith drew upon the shared faith experiences of both tragedy and triumph, grace and judgment, despair and hope.

I would suggest it is in light of these shared faith events that Katrina was "a storm of biblical proportions." As you hear the voices of those who experienced and continue to live the ravages of the hurricane and its aftermath, you will hear events echoing the biblical narrative – exodus, the passing through waters, the destruction, exile, return, and the beginning of restoration.

Just as Israel struggled to make sense of their shared experiences, so too are those who are living under the pall of Katrina's wrath. Just as Israel lamented and grieved, so too do those living in the aftermath of the storm. Just as Israel asked the pain-filled existential question, "Where is God?" so too is that deep yearning and soul-searching heard from the lips of those living in the wake of Katrina's raging destruction.

And just as God's people of old discovered in their time of loss and grief the strength, by God's ever-present grace, to go on and to re-build their cities and their lives, the people of God in this place and time are tapping into that same source of strength and hope. They also are bearing witness to the power of God's grace which is greater than any wind or raging water.

So I invite you to listen to the voices of those who have been forever changed by Katrina, "a storm of biblical proportions." Hear their journey of faith and doubt, of despair and hope. Listen to their experiences of exodus, flood, lament, exile, and return. Tune your ear to their cries and their loss. Let their words bear witness to the God who is with them – and with each of us – in the storms of life.

And by God's grace, join your voice and your hands with them, so that together, we might all one day see a day of restoration and new beginnings.

A Word About the Writings and the Writers

As a pastor living in Baton Rouge, LA – a community sixty-five miles from New Orleans – I have been overwhelmed by the incredible stories being told and lived in the aftermath of the storm. Everyone I've met in the days and months following Katrina's landfall has had powerful accounts of their experiences. Some are stories of despair and loss; others are of incredible generosity and hope. And still others are open-ended questions of meaning and faith.

I have come to realize, as I have listened to others and as I have told of my own experiences, the importance of the telling of the story for the recovery and healing process. I have also come to treasure the profound, meaningful witness of faith the stories represent. So I extended an invitation to my colleagues of the Evangelical Lutheran Church in America (ELCA) in ministry in south Louisiana to share (as they were willing and able) their "Katrina" stories. Their reflections gathered here span the approximate time period from August, 2005 to March, 2006.

The voices you will hear in this collection of writings (in addition to mine) are those of faith leaders in the ELCA – pastors, associates in ministry, youth ministers – who are serving in ministry in the greater New Orleans/Baton Rouge, Louisiana area. They are working with great courage and fortitude in very difficult times. I am grateful for their partnership, friendship, and willingness to share their stories.

Certainly, there are many other voices to be heard from many different faith traditions. And certainly the broad scope of the hurricane's destruction was not confined to southeast Louisiana. People in Mississippi, Alabama, Florida, western Louisiana, and east Texas were also affected. I anticipate that this is but one volume of many yet to come from many strands of the story.

There are also other words yet to be articulated – stories too raw and painful to speak just yet. One of the faith leaders responded to my invitation to write with this profound reply, "I think that I would find it extremely difficult to try and write a reflection regarding my Katrina experiences since I am still living it. This has been the most horrible thing that has happened in my life, and I am finding new little tragedies on a daily and weekly basis both personally and from others. So as I write this, I have to say that I am still processing these things internally and don't have it in my heart to put pen to paper regarding my experiences. I hope you understand."

Yes, dear reader, I hope you understand. Many more tears are yet to be shed. Many more stories are yet to be told. Much work is yet to be done.

But here is a beginning of the telling of one day and one word that changed everything:

August 29, 2005 ...   Katrina.

John McCullough Bade
Contributing Editor

Chapter 1
The Exodus

**Sign on Front Door of Christ the King Lutheran Church
Kenner, LA – August 28, 2005**

EMERGENCY!   Walt Ehrhardt

The Rev. Dr. Walton Ehrhardt serves as a Consultant to Bishop Paul Blom, Texas/Louisiana Gulf Coast Synod of the Evangelical Lutheran Church in America. Walt and family evacuated from New Orleans to the home of his oldest son in Alpharetta, GA on Saturday, August 27ᵗʰ, 2005. The families have since returned to their homes. One family temporarily resided with Walt in Mandeville (across Lake Ponchatrain from New Orleans on what is known as the "North Shore") as their home was being rebuilt. Jason and Anne Ehrhardt (Walt's son and daughter-in-law) and three children have returned to their damaged Metairie home to live in its upstairs level as the lower part of the house is rebuilt. Walt is assisting with pastoral care in the greater New Orleans metro area, counseling with people who have been displaced and are experiencing the many stresses of living through a disaster and its aftermath.

Some of us are fortunate enough to enjoy good health and good genes. As these and other blessings arrive at certain milestones in life, we are afforded the opportunity to reflect on meanings we generate over the passing of time. Friday, the 26ᵗʰ of August, 2005 was one such event for me.

It was my 65ᵗʰ birthday celebration. I feel like a "young" sixty-five. In all candor, I admit that I was having some difficulty approaching this milestone event which is so "colored" with prejudice in our contemporary culture. I wanted to enjoy my milestone in life with the people who are nearest and dearest to me – my family.

As my gift to myself, I had asked my New Orleans children and families (Allison, Jason, Jeremy) to join together for the dinner celebration at ZIA's in Metairie. (For any who are not familiar, ZIA's offers a fabulously diverse menu with superb cuisine to suit varied palates and yet reasonable on the wallet.) I wanted to "party!"

I did not want Mexican, and I did not want Italian. I wanted ZIA's Thai ribs! (I hope your gustatory senses are now at work!) I so anticipated this event. When 13 of us gather together, we have fun! The grandkids (ages 16, 12, 5, 3, and 1) provided the entertainment, and they were living up to the evening. Adults and kids were having a grand time, and my sentimental thoughts were for my Atlanta son and family who were not part of this party!

The food was being served as we noticed people around us focusing their attention on the TV screen located at our corner of the restaurant. The word "EMERGENCY" glared back at every pair of eyes. The governor was speaking, issuing her formal declaration of a "state of emergency!" We knew this "babe-KATRINA" was in the Gulf, and we did not want her fury to come our way. Hurricane Katrina in the Gulf of Mexico was not following the earlier forecast and was now endangering the Gulf coast.

At a particularly younger age and definitely more fool-hearty state of being, I had waited too long and learned it was too late to evacuate from Hurricane Camille. My "arrogant sense of being myself" (those were a colleague's words at that time) had decided to take my time, for after all, I had been through hurricanes before. I was in process of relocating from Biloxi to New Orleans at the time, where I was to begin my pastoral services as senior pastor of First English Lutheran Church. We rode out that horrific experience in our home, thirty-seven feet above sea level on the Back Bay of Biloxi. I can tell you about post-traumatic stress based on that experience alone. I vowed never do that again!!!

So in the face of those who have considered me "over-reactive," I have nonetheless advised my family to leave whenever a major hurricane enters the Gulf and targets New Orleans. They knew that would be the standard drill with me for Katrina. We would all evacuate, and connect the next morning to share each family's decision. We began to pray.

+ + +

Finding a Safe Haven   Sandra Barnes

*Associate in Ministry Sandra Barnes serves at Christ the
King Lutheran Church in Kenner, LA (a suburb of New
Orleans near the metropolitan airport). She has lived in the
New Orleans area all her life and has experienced a
mandatory evacuation order due to an approaching
hurricane three times – with Hurricanes George, Ivan and
Katrina. She and her family evacuated to Shreveport where
they lived for several months with family and friends.
Sandra's home in Slidell experienced water damage, and
they lost most of their possessions. They lived for several
weeks in a FEMA trailer parked in their driveway. As of
March 1, she and her family were "camping" in their home,
still making repairs.*

What a difference a month makes! At the August, 2005 council
meeting at Christ the King Lutheran Church, we were preparing for
the arrival of Pastor Ron Unger as our newly called pastor, and I was
preparing to hand off my duties as transitional pastor and step more
into an assistant role. I was looking forward to the plans we had for
Power Hour for the children, confirmation (especially our first
regional retreat), and youth plans. I was especially looking toward
Camp Hope and the ELCA Youth Gathering.

On a personal note, I was looking forward to beginning my classes
at Notre Dame Seminary in New Orleans and being an affiliate
student at Lutheran School of Theology in Chicago. My children
were starting back at school with all of their extracurricular
activities, and I was just getting to know my new students in my
classroom. My husband David and I, after having spent the weekend
at one of the Gulf Coast's resorts, were plotting how we could
arrange to have another getaway.

Then…Katrina…and everything changed. On August 26, the Friday
before the storm, I left school thinking about the GRE test I had to

retake. (My previous scores were too "old," how lovely.) I came home to find my husband trying to cut down a tall pine tree in our yard. When I asked him what he was doing, he told me, "The storm is heading right for us; you need to get ready." This meant pack and evacuate.

Normally, I had two safe havens, but neither person was available. We finally contacted my sister-in-law in Shreveport, LA, and I packed allergy medicine for my son, who is allergic to cats. (My sister-in-law has two of them which is why she wasn't higher on our call list, but I thought to myself that we would only be there a few days and could just "fake" it.)

Saturday, August 27, was spent taking the GRE – I learned that testing will go on, evacuation orders or not – as well as making frantic phone calls. I talked to the church council president, and we concurred that people needed to get out. We decided we would not have worship services on Sunday, August 28, but we were confident we would be back together the following weekend. I packed the car, took the kids, and left my husband to stay. David is an engineer for WDSU, one of the local television stations, and he had to be there to help cover the news.

I spent most of Sunday worried about David. Cell phone lines were melting down rapidly, so communication was beginning its descent into chaos. The more I heard about the storm, the more frightened I became. I knew the kids and I were safe, but David was going to be at the transmitter in Chalmette, LA. Many people now know about the devastation that hit that area of Louisiana, and he was supposed to stay there and work. He finally called me late Sunday night to tell me that the station was moving its headquarters to Jackson, MS, and he would be getting out of New Orleans after all. My first prayer was answered.

David was able to meet us in Shreveport, and I was so thankful to God when I saw him pull up in the driveway. Normally the drive would take about four to five hours, but because of the evacuation traffic, he made it there in fourteen hours. We at least had a little while to be together, and we were together when everything just came apart.

We all watched in horror the news. Over and over again, the images were replayed; and like many others, we just couldn't watch any more. On Tuesday, August 30, David had to go back to get equipment back online so they could report the news to everyone, and I had to focus on my calling.

+ + +

A City of Shelters   Robin McCullough-Bade

Pastor Robin McCullough-Bade (my wife) began her work as interim pastor at the Lutheran Church of Our Saviour in Baton Rouge, LA on September 1, 2005 – the week of Katrina.   We live and serve as ELCA pastors in Baton Rouge.

As you will read, the city of Baton Rouge experienced the impact of the evacuation. Estimates are that Baton Rouge (a city of approximately 250,000 pre-Katrina) doubled in size overnight as evacuees fled New Orleans.   A survey conducted by the sociology department at Louisiana State University found that over one-half of all homes in Baton Rouge had evacuees living in them – some for several months.

Robin recounts the experience of Katrina's impact for us as a family and as a community.

Urgent warnings about the approaching of Hurricane Katrina towards New Orleans area were blasted throughout the Gulf Coast region. "Leave immediately!"

Over a million people evacuated from New Orleans and nearby communities, heeding the advice of leaders. Hundreds of thousands of vehicles passed through Baton Rouge as people desperately tried to move beyond harm's way.   Many evacuees stopped at Baton Rouge, staying with family and friends.   They brought pets, a few clothes, some favorite items, and coolers filled with food from their refrigerators.   All of us prepared to wait out the storm during the next days.

Our family diligently gathered supplies – ice, batteries, water, canned goods, and other basics.   Sunday was a such a beautiful day.

Who would have guessed a storm was brewing? Despite the blue skies, we taped up the windows and secured any possible flying objects. We pondered the best places to park our cars so both of them would not be crushed by the same tree. Throughout our preparations, we paused to ask each other, "What might this night bring?"

As darkness descended Sunday night, August 28, 2005, we called out-of-state relatives who were concerned about our decision to stay at home. We felt safe; Baton Rouge was not in the range of the category five Hurricane Katrina. They promised to pray for us.

We chose a small corner room of our house to wait out the storm. In the darkness of night, we listened to the howling wind, knowing we should sleep while we could. Yet, how could one sleep? As the night progressed, the whirls and howls of the winds increased, creating a noise level so loud that sleeping became impossible. The sharp snapping of branches of nearby trees was followed by the resounding crash of limbs upon the ground or buildings.

We lost electricity in the early hours of morning before dawn's first light. In the darkness, we waited and prayed. That's all we could do. We lit our candles. And then we waited and prayed some more.

Finally, dawn came. We looked out at the bending of trees. Now we could visually track the snapping of tree branches with the crashing of limbs upon the ground. Some branches danced to the sky before being yanked to the ground, unwilling to leave their tree trunk. The movement of wind, branches and trees was an intense struggle.

Eventually, the storm calmed. Neighbors came out to access the war zone on our street. Most of the homes avoided massive damage. Neighbors gathered together for meals as we ate our way through the thawing food in our freezers. Outside propane grills served as our stoves. Daily we strategized and coordinated our searches for ice, food, and gasoline.

Just when it appeared New Orleans was breathing a sigh of relief, the news came that levees had broken open. Massive flooding covered neighborhoods and communities. A second evacuation occurred. This one did not go as well.

For us, our electricity at our home was off for five days. It seemed a minor inconvenience compared to what so many were enduring. Each night we lit candles and gathered on the patio to watch the local newscasts on our battery-operated television. We literally hovered over that four-inch black-and-white screen, trying to see the faces of the stranded people. There they were on bridges and rooftops, begging for help. Why didn't we see a massive rescue on this little screen?

At night, we tried to sleep in the heat of our home and on our patio, but it was hard not to think of those who were also trying to sleep elsewhere in that same oppressive heat. Yet those people slept on rooftops, praying for rescue, food and water. Normally, the stars and moon of the sky have been a source of comfort for me; but on those nights, they became a haunting witness to those in need. There was nothing normal about those nights – not with so many people stranded.

Baton Rouge continued to overflow with people. New Orleans residents were coming and going, seeking loved ones, checking on their homes and businesses. FEMA, the Red Cross workers, volunteers of all shapes and sizes, and the media came to our city. The grocery stores could not keep fresh fruits and vegetables. Other stores were depleted of pillows, sheets, underwear; and the list goes on. Shelves became empty. Chaos reigned.

Raw stories of pain and devastating loss filled each hour. One evacuee explained, "I have nothing. I no longer have nail clippers. I have to replace everything I have owned in my life."

Baton Rouge became a city of shelters. The large convention center in the city became a refuge for thousands. Churches large and small throughout the area opened their doors.

And most amazingly, over half of the Baton Rouge homes became shelters, not just for days, but weeks and months. One man had nineteen people in his home in addition to his family of four. Most of them he had never met before Katrina. They stayed weeks. This man came to a meeting of faith leaders wearing a cross. "I am a Christian, but these people are not leaving. How do I feed them on my salary? They can't access their bank accounts. All has been lost. What can I do?" His kind heart was breaking under stress and exhaustion.

A pall settled over Baton Rouge and the whole area. Yet, the key story of Baton Rouge during the hours, days, weeks and months after Hurricane Katrina was the response of the faith community. This disaster was bigger than all the relief agencies combined. All of us became first responders. How could we not? One shelter manager in one of the smaller churches was asked to explain why her congregation became a shelter. A look of utter bewilderment filled her face. Her answer was simple and filled with peace, "We are Christians."

No other answer was needed.

"'Lord, when was it that we saw you hungry and gave you food, or thirsty and gave you something to drink? And when was it that we saw you a stranger and welcomed you, or naked and gave you clothing?'"

"'Truly I tell you, just as you did it to one of the least of these who are members of my family, you did it to me.'" (Matthew 25: 37-38, 40 NRSV)

+ + +

"I Didn't Even Bring My Bible!"   John McCullough Bade

His broad shoulders and stout build suggested a different occupation in his earlier years. I discovered later that Brother Leroy played for the Chicago Bears before turning in his cleats to join a different team.

Brother Leroy is a pastor in the African Methodist Episcopal (AME) Church. He and his family had hurriedly evacuated his home in New Orleans East as the storm approached. His exodus brought him to Baton Rouge, and his clergy connections led him to a hastily organized meeting of faith leaders.

He listened intently to the reports from representatives of FEMA and the Red Cross – how to apply for assistance, where immediate resources could be found.   The information was crucial, he knew.

When the reports were done, Brother Leroy slowly raised himself, straightening the broad human frame bent down with the weight of the disaster. In a quiet, raspy voice, he began to tell his exodus story. He told of the great throng of people trying to leave all at once. He told of the growing anxiety and fear that swept over his neighborhood as the storm spun nearer and nearer. He told of the last-minute decision to leave.

And then he paused, casts his eyes downward, and quietly said, "You've got to understand – we've lost everything. Everything." He shook his head, heavy with weariness. "I didn't even bring my Bible! I've got to preach next Sunday. How is a preacher supposed to preach without his Bible?"

Through his agony, Brother Leroy gave flesh and blood to the pain and suffering of the day. Through his quiet words, he articulated the loss and struggle of hundreds of thousands. Through his presence, Brother Leroy gave witness to his faith in a God who suffered loss on a cross – a God who travels the exodus journey.

Even without his Bible, Brother Leroy preached the Word the following Sunday.

And he preached the Word that afternoon at that meeting – the Word made flesh in his Saviour and Lord, and the Word made visible in Leroy that day.

+ + +

Exodus   **Walton Ehrhardt**

The Exodus story is a faith story. It, too, narrates a massive evacuation. It, too, is a story of deliverance. The Exodus story of the Scriptures has been one of my foundational stories about human life and our connection with the divine in human existence. As a "faith person," I have always taught my children this story as one of heroic proportion that challenges the human condition.

Walking forward into the unknown in the confidence that we are not alone on the journey is a constant source of strength and comfort. One must take one day at a time on the journey. That is the core of the psychoanalytic work we undertake with each patient, couple, family, and group.

Saturday morning, August 27, 2005 at about 6 a.m., my daughter Allison called. She and her family were leaving for Mobile to stay with her father-in-law in the old family home built of foot-thick concrete walls on high ground in old Mobile. I long-distanced my son, Jonathan, in Atlanta to inform him and his wife of the events. The welcome mat was out for our refuge, and the invitation extended to the other siblings. Jason and Anne and the kids, Jeremy and Shannon (and their yet unborn), my wife Carol and I would head for Atlanta.

By 12:30 on Saturday afternoon, we all were on the road. Our exodus had begun. The drive to Atlanta, in and of itself, was easy. Traffic was incredibly "light" until we reached the entry points where highway repair slowed everything to a crawl. By midnight we had all arrived, safely, at our destination.

None of us knew what events were to befall a vast area and a multitude of people. We did not know that within the ensuing thirty-six hours, our definition of "normal" would change forever.

+ + +

The Kindness of Strangers   Bob Hildebrandt

Pastor Bob Hildebrandt is a retired ELCA pastor living in Metairie (a suburb of New Orleans). Bob has lived in the New Orleans area since 1967 and served as pastor of St. Mark Lutheran Church, Metairie, LA for thirty years. He also served as a chaplain in the LA National Guard and retired as State Chaplain with rank of Colonel. His home suffered wind and rain damage with about an inch of water in two-thirds of the house. (The flood waters from the levee breach stopped two houses down from his home.)

Bob and his wife Beverly were able to stay in their home most of the time while battling the mold, sheet rock and roof damage, and downed fences and trees. They evacuated to Lafayette, LA (about 125 miles northwest of New Orleans) where they experienced the kindness of strangers.

We have all heard about welcoming strangers.

Part of our family was on the receiving end of this lesson. At five in the morning, Sunday August 28th, we joined the contraflow (the reversal of the east-bound lanes of I-10 out of New Orleans) going west on the east-bound I-10. Our caravan consisted of two vans: in one was my wife, Bev, myself, and three grandchildren; in the other was our daughter-in-law, one grandchild, and their dog.

I was to facilitate a call consultant session at the Lutheran Church of Our Saviour in Baton Rouge, LA (65 miles northwest of New Orleans) that morning. We needed to go west to avoid the storm anyway, and we thought maybe Baton Rouge would be far enough away. After the service and meeting, we received a gracious invitation to stay in a home in Baton Rouge; but it looked like the storm could strike there as well. We decided to go further west.

As we drove Interstate 10, I called First Lutheran Church in Lafayette, LA (about 60 miles west of Baton Rouge). The person who answered said, "Of course, you would be welcome to stay in the church." When we pulled into the parking lot of the church, a member was waiting for us and offered for us stay there. We were also informed that a family up the road had a pot of spaghetti on and had an upstairs where we could stay and be more comfortable.

We went to the house and met for the first time the family of Steve and Karen DuBlois. After enjoying the meal, we accepted their offer of taking all seven of us total strangers in. We found a kennel nearby for the dog and took the two bedrooms and bath upstairs for what we expected to be a couple of days of evacuation. It turned into nearly four weeks.

The angels in this story were, of course, the DuBlois family. Our oldest granddaughter, Veronica (age 11), reflecting on the experience a week or so after getting home put it dramatically: "Karen and Steve really saved our lives." I think we could have survived otherwise; but this couple, members of First Lutheran Church in Lafayette, certainly helped us in a time of need. The children and adults received a blessing and will remember that we were strangers taken in by angels.

+ + +

Chapter 2
Passing Through the Waters

A Home in Lakeview September 11, 2005

Pharaoh's Armies   John McCullough Bade

From distant rooftops, their cries rang out –
      "The waters are rising!"
      "The house is washing away!"
      "Help us!"

In cavernous domes, their pleas echoed –
      "Where is food? Where is water?"
      "Where are the buses?"
      "Help us!"

In corridors dark, their voices whispered –
      "We have no power."
      "Patients are dying."
      "Help us!"

In desperate days, their empty glances spoke when words failed –
      "We've lost everything."
      "Nothing is left."
      "Nothing."
      "Help us!"

How long, O Lord, how long?

When will help come?
      When will resources arrive?
         When will they know promised relief?

Yet again, the wheels of Pharaoh's chariot turn slowly,
      stuck in the muck and mud and mire
      of paperwork and politics,
      of old paradigms and inflexible policy,
      of long-established strategies and unyielding bureaucracies.

And still, their cries ring out.

When There Are No Words   Robin McCullough-Bade

The following is the first sermon Robin preached as interim pastor on September 4, 2005 – the first Sunday after Katrina.

Grace and peace to you from Jesus Christ our risen Lord.

We begin with a reading from Psalm 46:
God is our refuge and strength, a very present help in trouble. Therefore we will not fear, though the earth should change, though the mountains shake in the heart of the sea; though its waters roar and foam, though the mountains tremble with its tumult .... Be still, and know that I am God! I am exalted among the nations, I am exalted in the earth. The Lord of hosts is with us; the God of Jacob is our refuge. (Psalm 46: 1-3; 10-11 NRSV)

Let us pray. Gracious and mighty God, we have been witnesses to the power of a hurricane to level a city. Send your Spirit to console our breaking hearts. Give us courage, strength, and guidance; in Christ we pray. Amen.

It is overwhelming. There are simply no words to describe the events of this week.

The week began with warnings of a hurricane. The winds, rains, floods and power outages came. And when it was over, New Orleans breathed a sign of relief. The city and surrounding area was hit hard but had survived Katrina.

Then came the truly bad news. The levees were breaking. The city was flooding. The looting of stores had begun. Violence was spreading.

Then, the news got worse. Relief was slow in coming. The water was becoming contaminated with sewage, gas, and other products.

After four days, some hospitals were not yet evacuated. People were now housed in our gyms, churches, hotels, with friends, family, and strangers.

The stories of the survivors have been incredible. The images on televisions continue to be staggering.

Make no mistake: we have witnessed horrific devastation. We have witnessed suffering and pain of staggering proportions. We have witnessed scenes which we cannot forget or turn our backs on.

Indeed, we have witnessed the words of Psalm 46. We have seen the earth change. We have seen the waters roar and foam.

It is overwhelming. There are simply no words to describe the events of this week.

Questions seem insurmountable. Where do you move 1,000,000 people? How do you feed them? Where do they sleep? What jobs will they have? How do you educate their children and youth? How does life go on?

These are not distant, remote questions concerning strangers. Some of those who are left homeless are colleagues, loved ones, and relatives. Some are the poorest of the poor. Some are orphans, too young to tell of their next of kin.

It is overwhelming. There are simply no words to describe the events of this week.

So what do we do when there are no words? What can be said when we are left speechless? What happens when we are left with only our sighs?

Romans 8:26 describes these times: *"Likewise the Spirit helps us in our weakness. . . . but that very Spirit intercedes with sighs too deep for words." (NRSV)*

So, we drop to our knees and thank God for coming to us in our times of weakness when we have sighs too deep for words. We receive God's presence as a gift from a loving, compassionate God.

Maybe some day – one day – our sighs will be turned into words, for words help us name the trauma of these days. Words help give shape to the pain and agony in our hearts, spirits, and minds. Words become part of the healing process. Words connect us with others who have had similar experiences.

As we seek words to describe what has occurred this week, know there is an essential word to be proclaimed here today. It is the Word of God made known in Jesus Christ. It is the Word of God which consoles us and gives us hope.

"In the beginning was the Word, and the Word was with God, and the Word was God." (John 1:1 NRSV)

That Word is Jesus Christ.

"In him was life, and life was the light of all people. The light shines in the darkness, and the darkness did not overcome it." (John 1:5 NRSV)

Christ came into our world, suffered immensely, and gave his life. Yet, death could not defeat Christ. For that matter, Hurricane Katrina could not defeat Christ. The light of Christ still shines. God is here, present as our consolation and hope. The psalmist had it right: God is our refuge and strength. God is a very present help in trouble.

And so we begin the days of sacred storytelling. We tell about this week – a week set apart like all others in our lives. We tell our stories. We listen to others tell their stories.

In the speaking of these words, we become knit together by our words, our sighs, and our tears. In the speaking of these words, we become connected to one another, and we realize our shared humanity – our need for God and our need for one another in the coming days, weeks, months, and years.

We speak; and we listen.

Yet we as the church will be called upon to do more than listen to each other's stories. We will be called upon to seek ways to respond to people in their deepest needs. No doubt, we will continue to be stretched as a faith community to embody God's Word of love.

We, the church, have always been a people of the story. Now that story gets lived through us in acts of love and compassion. Now we, the church, become the story of God's love to others.

For some who have lost their homes, possessions, loved ones, jobs, and dreams in this hurricane, all they have left is their story. They will struggle for the rest of their lives to find the words to describe the events of this week – events that have changed the course of their lives – as they seek to find the ways to rebuild their lives.

We certainly have been united by Hurricane Katrina, a mighty hurricane. But before there was a Hurricane Katrina, we were united by Jesus Christ.

Bishop Hanson, presiding bishop of the ELCA puts it this way: "As we hear the heartbreaking stories of people who are suffering and dying from this disaster, we are reminded of refugees throughout the world. Please pray for all who struggle and suffer from the injustices of hunger, homelessness, and despair. I ask you to join me in renewing our commitment as Lutherans to be present wherever there is suffering, to bring healing and hope in Jesus' name." *(Statement from Bishop Mark Hanson, Evangelical Lutheran Church in America, sent via email September 2, 2005)*

And so, when we are unable to speak words – when the pain and suffering leaves us silent and sighing – we turn to God's Word.

We end – and begin – with God's word from Romans 8: *"For I am convinced that neither death, nor life, nor angels, nor rulers, nor things present, nor things to come, nor powers, nor height, nor depth, nor anything else in all creation will be able to separate us from the love of God in Christ Jesus our Lord." (Romans 8:38-39 NRSV)*

And let the word be spoken: "It is so. Amen"

+ + +

Communicating the Reality   Walton Ehrhardt

Walt communicates the challenge of communication in the midst of the storm.

"EXODUS!" This headline on the Saturday morning August 27 issue of the Times Picayune (the New Orleans newspaper) greeted every reader. We all know about the massive exit from the city. We have followed the story of tragedy, death, anarchy, and devastation.

Those of us who are professionally trained in counseling have some understanding about psychic development, regression, denial, and malignant greed. We know about projective identification and paranoid/schizoid states of mind. We attempt to expand our understanding of unconscious dynamics that affect groups, large and small. Basic assumption processes of dependence, pairing, fight/flight, and incohesion which leads to aggregation and massification – all are technical, identifiable ways of articulating the madness that has taken place and continues in our lives.

"You cannot go back!"

No psychological, clinical words are needed to interpret this message. These are harsh-sounding words to have to hear, and harsher still to have to speak.

Children do not understand those words very well. My three-year-old grandson told his mom, "Our house is broke. God told me." Children cannot comprehend the after-effects of a disaster. Most adults know the apres coup (the lasting effects) of their choices. Many have died because of their decisions. There is anger and blame. What matters most is that people learn from the full measure of lessons that life teaches.

The reality is: it's difficult these days to communicate the reality. The immensity of the devastation – the enormous need on so many levels – it is almost impossible to convey in words.

I no longer curse computers. Now I thank God for the technology of computer and internet. It has been the vehicle for our connection and communication with others. No, I no longer curse computers. Cell phones, however, now they are another story. They were rendered virtually useless in the storm. I cursed my cell phone. "You *****!!! 'Can you hear me now?' 'No!!!' 'Can you hear me now?'"

Yes, communication is critical these days. It's what keeps us going. Ever time one of us receives an e-mail addressed "Dear...," that one word carries such a depth of meanings! Your care and concern for our well-being and your messages offering us support have been indelibly imprinted on our hearts and souls.

We will be asking for your assistance in more specific ways as our needs are revealed to us. And we will continue to attempt to communicate to you the reality in which we now live.

+ + +

Communication Chaos   Sandra Barnes

Sandra writes of the importance of staying in contact with congregational members and loved ones – and the importance of prayer – in the aftermath of the storm.

The first focus once we had all safely evacuated was establishing lines of communication, especially with an unstable cellular phone system.   Having nothing else, I turned to the internet and emailed the few people whose addresses I remembered.   Through the fantastic network of friends, I was able to relay information to congregational members and friends as to how members were doing, where to find help (such as LA Purchase disaster assistance, FEMA, Red Cross), and how to connect with the synod office. And I tried to pass on bits of encouragement.

To all of those people who emailed me or called me in those first days – THANK YOU!!!   You became a vital resource as we ministered to each other as a scattered people of God!   The emails eventually evolved back into a more normal newsletter with readings and thoughts, and I was able to forward Pastor Unger's first sermon to everyone via the email!

With each email and, increasingly, with each phone call, we reconnected, we were encouraged by each other in the Spirit, and we became empowered as we faced the new challenges before us in ministry.

I also received literally hundreds of emails from around the country, lifting us in prayer and offering to help us with time, talents, and gifts.   It has been so moving to experience the outpouring of love from our brothers and sisters in Christ.   It was a very concrete reminder that we are all one Body.

On the other side of communication, I worked with the synod office passing on information as I could, especially reports from my husband who was "there" for most of it due to his responsibilities at WDSU. Sometimes communication was a bit more than I selfishly wanted; I would hear reports from my husband about the "armed escorts" he had to get going to work in New Orleans, as well as the sickening details about the damage to our home and neighborhood.

As phone communications improved, I talked at length with many of our members, rejoicing in their safety, rejoicing in the news that our church facility was for the most part spared damage. Talking and listening seemed to be what most of us needed – someone who would just listen to our particular stories, and be a loving presence.

+ + +

All in the Boat Together   John McCullough Bade

As the levees failed and the waters overtook the city of New Orleans, boats became critical in the rescue efforts.   Who could have envisioned that the Louisiana Department of Wildlife and Fisheries would play such a crucial role in those critical first days?   But they had ready access to boats and were quickly mobilized.

The boat has often been used as a symbol for the Church.   Somehow, that makes profound sense since the storm.

Robin and I led worship at the Lutheran Church of the Galilean in La Place, LA (just outside New Orleans) Sunday, September 11, 2005 – two weeks after Katrina hit.   The logo for this congregation is a boat with a cross as its mast (a significant imagery, as you will soon see).   Entry to city of New Orleans was still restricted.   Residents from some areas were allowed to "look and leave," while many other sections of the city were still completely closed.   La Place was the closest community "open."

We didn't know what to expect when we drove the fifty miles from Baton Rouge to the church.   We didn't know what damage the sanctuary had experienced; we didn't know if people would be able to get to the church.   As was the case for so much in those days, we just didn't know.

People began to arrive, eager to be together to pray, to be nourished in Word and Sacrament, to listen, and to tell their stories.   We had developed a liturgy of bidding prayers and remembrance; and as people arrived, we asked for volunteers to assist with the readings.

We soon realized that many in the congregation didn't know one other.   It became clear that there were people gathered from all over the city.   Some had driven forty miles to gather for worship that Sunday.   As we inquired during the announcements, we discovered there were members from at least eight congregations – ELCA and Missouri Synod Lutherans – present.

Strangers were strangers no more. Lines of division were erased. Barriers of denomination, ethnicity, race, and class were knocked down.

Yes, it's true. The boat is critical in rescue and recovery efforts. In destructive waters, the boat is the vessel of life and hope.

So, too, is the Church the vessel of life and hope, providing safety, refuge, and peace amidst the raging waters.

+ + +

The Second Wave   Anton Kern

Pastors Anton Kern and Sean Ewbank serve at Hosanna Lutheran Church in Mandeville, LA (on the "North Shore" – one of the communities across Lake Ponchatrain from New Orleans). Mandeville experienced wind and storm damage from uprooted trees and pounding rains. The church building experienced minimal damage and became a staging area for volunteers.

Anton and his family evacuated to Houston, TX during the storm, while Sean remained in Mandeville. Anton was able to get back to Mandeville a week after Katrina hit, and the congregation worshiped with 90 in attendance September 4 (with no air conditioning or electrical power) .

Anton grew up in New Orleans and knows the area and its culture well. He sent a series of updates to family and friends as the relief and recovery efforts began. The following is an update sent October 4, 2005 – five weeks after the storm.

When a hurricane hits, the destruction begins and then is followed by a period of calm as the eye passes over. These past weeks have been like the eye of the hurricane. We began to survey the physical damage and plan ways to restore damaged homes and property. After the eye passes over, the winds reverse direction and resume their destruction. I believe the eye is about to pass over us, and we are about to see the destruction that shows itself in financial and emotional impact which may be a greater challenge than the physical damage.

We are seeing more and more people from St. Bernard Parish (a parish in Louisiana is the same as a county everywhere else) who have moved into our community. Some are living with friends, relatives or kind strangers. Others have secured a residence and plan to stay here. Recent news accounts from St. Bernard officials indicate that there is not one habitable house, no functioning businesses, therefore no taxes; and unless there is federal aid, there will be no money to pay police and other essential workers. Many New Orleans school system workers and city workers will soon be jobless as leaders attempt to balance budgets. The state of Louisiana announced that they have to cut one billion dollars from the budget to pay for Katrina, which surely means job cuts.

The job situation remains uncertain for many of our people. We are discovering that some key members are permanently moved.

The ministry opportunities are enormous. We are trusting that just as leaders have moved to other cities, new leaders will emerge from those folks who have moved into our community.

The emotional toll is beginning to surface, too. We are thankful that Dr. Walt Ehrhardt has been assigned by Bishop Paul Blom to help us through that second wave of effects of Katrina. Walt has already met with our junior and senior high youth and is scheduled to meet with adults as well. We anticipate that the initial meeting will result in ongoing conversations as we explore the unfolding of the "new normal."

Even though we are about to face the financial and emotional impact of Katrina, we still believe that God is calling us to serve as a staging place for hands to help put together the physical aspects of life.

We believe we have an open door to reach people for Christ and help engage them in a deeper spiritual journey. Uncertainty remains as to whether we will have the finances and people with the emotional resources necessary to seize this extraordinary ministry opportunity.

+ + +

Chapter 3
Exile

FEMA Trailers in Baton Rouge - October, 2005

The Scattered Flock

Ron Unger

Pastor Ron Unger was serving as pastor at The Lutheran Church of the Galilean in La Place, LA (20 miles northwest of New Orleans) when Katrina hit. He had just accepted a new call to Christ the King Lutheran Church in Kenner, LA (a suburb of New Orleans), and his farewell Sunday at Galilean was to have been September 4th, the Sunday after Katrina hit. Instead, he presided at an informal service of Holy Communion in the lobby of the hotel in Jackson, MS where he and his extended family had taken up refuge from the storm.

Ron's home was in Chalmette, LA in St. Bernard Parish – an area devastated by the storm and its aftermath. The house and all its possessions were destroyed.

The following is the sermon Ron "preached" on September 11, 2005. It was his first sermon at his new call at Christ the King and was delivered by email to his new, scattered congregation.

Grace, mercy and peace to you from God the Father and from our Lord and Savior Jesus Christ!

This is my first sermon as your new pastor.   What a strange beginning! I'm not standing in the pulpit (even though we've heard it's dry) but sitting in a motel in Jackson, MS. Last Sunday, instead of leading worship at The Lutheran Church of the Galilean in La Place for the final time, I conducted worship for about 35 evacuees in the motel lobby. For the Holy Communion we used a bagel left over from the complimentary continental breakfast and a plastic "Super 8 Motel" cup as a chalice.

Who would have thought that anything could upstage the anniversary of 9/11? But here we are, preoccupied with our own losses and disruption of lives due to Hurricane Katrina.

We are the church wherever we have been scattered by recent events. It will be awhile before we can congregate with each other in Kenner; but congregation or not, we are always the church.

At present we are in "diaspora." I'm told that is a term familiar to many of our members. It means we are dispersed, as were the children of God after the destruction of Jerusalem in the 6th century BC and as were the early Christians fleeing the persecution of Rome.

St. Peter addressed his first letter to people similar to us. *"To the exiles of the Dispersion. . . who have been chosen and destined by God the Father and sanctified by the Spirit to be obedient to Jesus Christ...."* *(1 Peter 1:1-2 NRSV)*

That's who we are too! We need that reminder. After hearing so much bad news and seeing it on the TV screen, we need all the good news we can get.

Peter reminds suffering people whose faith and hope are being greatly tested, who might even be tempted to think that God has abandoned them, *"You are a chosen race, a royal priesthood, a holy nation, God's own people."* *(I Peter 2:9 NRSV)*

Some of our folks have heard news that their homes were preserved. Others of us weren't as fortunate. (My home in Chalmette is still under water. I'm hoping to relocate to La Place soon.) Most of us have learned that family members and loved ones are safe. Some of us still fear what may have happened to people we know and love. Some of us have been traumatized by horrific events; but most of us have been overwhelmed by God's love made evident in the "kindness of strangers."

There will be continued tests of our faith, hope, and love. So Peter speaks to that as well. *"Humble yourselves therefore under the mighty hand of God, so that he may exalt you in due time. Cast all your anxiety on him, because he cares for you. Discipline yourselves, keep alert. Like a roaring lion your adversary the devil prowls around, looking for someone to devour. Resist him, steadfast in your faith, for you know that your brothers and sisters in all the world are undergoing the same kinds of suffering. And after you have suffered for a little while, the God of all grace, who has called you to his eternal glory in Christ, will himself restore, support, strengthen, and establish you."*
(1 Peter 5:6-10 NRSV)

And the peace of God which passes all understanding keep your hearts and minds in Christ Jesus. Amen.

P.S. As I hope you will soon learn, my sermons are usually a bit longer than this.

+ + +

Dispersed! Walton Ehrhardt

Walt reflects on "life in exile," written September 6, 2005.

Life in the "*diaspora.*" My thoughts turn to the old stories of the Scriptures, those stories of the children of Israel living in the diaspora. Yes, externally in the physical world much of life was harsh and not familiar.

New places ... new people... something that history has demonstrated repeatedly ... lessons that conquerors learned and applied to the conquered: divide the people and disperse them to break their spirit and their will. "Massification" of any traumatized group becomes an almost automatic defensive function. The vanquished will then be more easily assimilated into their new culture and surroundings.

But the *spirit* is not so easily broken. The inner world continues to be a mystery. That marvelous book by Anna Maria Rizzuto, <u>The Birth of the Living God,</u> seems to echo what I am observing and personally experiencing. The function and purpose defensively in the psyche is defensive and intended to give hope in the face of despair. It is a relationship that is repeated over and over, and again and again – chiefly in the Psalms: *"God is my refuge and my strength, a very present help in time of trouble." (Ps. 46:1 NSRV)* In the eyes of the Christian faithful, *" In all things, God is at work for your good...." (Romans 5 NSRV)*

We have met and made wonderful new friends here in Alpharetta, GA, this "community of saints." Our beloved Jonathan and Chardel and sons have opened their home to us. We are seventeen in all (plus four cats and four dogs)! With their neighbors and friends, they have come together around us, clothed us, sheltered us and our pets-in-exile, fed us, connected us with schools, and even opened job opportunities!

We have become connected as a family in such intimately painful yet caring honesty this week! Living in exile is never easy, especially when the reality is becoming painfully clear that some of us will be speaking the words to children, "We cannot go back."

My son Jeremy and I drove to our North Shore (St.Tammany Parish) homes in Mandeville yesterday. It was Labor Day. We went to review the fruits of our labors. The devastation spreads far beyond New Orleans. (The area affected is comparable to the geographical area of Great Britain, can you believe???)

Our homes did _not_ flood. The wind damage is horrible. To our delight, our homes are fine. I will need a chimney on my house and a chain saw to take care of the fifteen trees that were destroyed. None of these huge monsters fell on our house. Thankful!! (I told Jeremy he needs to cut the grass, and he told me that I haven't told him that since high school.)   There are neighbors whose houses were _destroyed._ Just one of those centenarian Ponderosa pines can crush a house and reduce one's home to rubble in one fell swoop. Four of my neighbors experienced that loss.

Infrastructure still stinks! Even though we were able to go back to see the condition of our houses, we can't return home until the officials tell us that everything is "open." Unfortunately there is looting, pillaging as the enviously "sick" prey upon us in our boundary-vulnerable brokenness.

Allison and David have learned that water intruded in their house, and they lost the car left behind. They have enrolled the two girls in school here. Elizabeth is in her second year of high school and Madeline is a seventh grader. Neither is taking this well, as is to be expected. Today, David (a teacher) was hired as a resource teacher in the high school. Allison has a job interview as a specialized care nurse on Monday. Things are looking good for them.

Jason and Anne will be moving into temporary quarters here. His pharmaceutical company has assured him of support and employment. Little Jack (5 years old) started kindergarten today.

The house is less crowded and certainly more quiet. Yes, there is gratitude for the joyous sounds children introduce each day; but when they are tired and cranky, you yearn for a "space apart."

Jeremy and Shannon (two months pregnant) have taken space in an extended stay hotel since he has been temporarily assigned to the Atlanta Secret Service field office – yet another of the intriguing "God signs" that are marking our way on the journey and giving lifts to our sagging spirits. God is indeed our refuge and strength!

I have been networking through the professional membership organizations to which I belong and am affiliated. Those connections are most helpful, and the connections support hope! The desire to counter the helplessness is at times "crazy-making." I want to do some kind of work in response to the crises. The Southeastern Synod of the Evangelical Lutheran Church in America wants my services ASAP. I'll check in there and begin work tomorrow. I also have two patients and two supervisees now connected by phone. Life is continuing.

+ + +

The Hidden Blessings

Jim Shears

Pastor Jim Shears has served as pastor at Gethsemane Lutheran Church in Chalmette, LA (St. Bernard Parish) since 1993. Chalmette is one of the hardest-hit areas in the storm, and the church building at Gethsemane had over eight feet of water in it. Jim and his family lost their home and possessions in Chalmette. They evacuated to the Atlanta area to a Presbyterian congregation where they stayed for about a month. His wife Aloma was offered a job in Memphis, TN, and the family moved there to begin again.

Jim continues to serve as pastor at Gethsemane, commuting from Memphis. He has a FEMA trailer in the church parking lot in which he stays when in Chalmette. Jim has gone to where the scattered members are located and has gathered them for worship in Baton Rouge and in Kenner.

The congregation has set up a tent with a wooden floor and worshiped for the first time onsite on Palm Sunday (April 9, 2006). The congregation was scattered from North Carolina to Oregon. Most have found their way back to Louisiana and Mississippi; some are in the New Orleans area. As of February 28, 2006, 90 percent of the pre-Katrina residents of St. Bernard parish had been unable to return to their homes.

Jim's writings reflect the hope and resiliency of the members and residents of the parish.

Evacuating was the most difficult decision to make. We had done it once before, and nothing happened. We had dodged several "bullets" and had even ridden out Hurricane Cindy. Leaving is such a hassle, not to mention expensive. But Sunday morning, we knew we had to go. After all, our neighbors across the street, who have never left, were packing up.

Obviously, we are glad we did. I remember sitting in a church office in Atlanta after the storm, looking at unbelievable images of our community on television. We even found on the screen our house, the high school, Aloma's workplace – all under water. I turned to Aloma, still in shock, and said, "God's gonna find a way to bless us in this."

And God has. We have been blessed way beyond anything that we lost. Her work situation, Jonathan's school, Joshua's opportunities, and my prospects for ministry are all very much different than they were – and better. Our view of the future is very positive.

The first time I was able to gather some of Gethsemane's members together, in three different locations, I asked them to share one way God had blessed them since the storm. It was a blatant attempt to get them to look on the positive side of things. I heard things about the chance to start over, about the wonderful people God had put in people's paths, and about what churches had done. There were a lot of tears as people remembered the loss and talked about God's grace.

One story was particularly amazing. Bill (a member of the congregation whose house is in Chalmette) and a co-worker went back to Bill's house to see what it was like and what they could salvage. They went to the front door, but couldn't open it because of the mud. They tried the garage door, but it wouldn't budge. They went to the back door. Mud, again! So they went through a window in the breakfast nook. While Bill was looking around at the mess and trying to deal with the smell, his co-worker, who was not a Christian, picked up a small plaque that had been on the wall. It was on the floor and had somehow been spared the mud. He said to Bill, "Bill, you need to see this." Visibly shaken, he handed the plaque to Bill. It read, "When God closes a door, he opens a window."

Bill broke down, and his co-worker's life was changed. Bill had a hard time telling the story, but he said he had never felt the presence of God so strongly, right there in the middle of life's biggest mess.

I have had other occasions to gather some of the folks together – at Thanksgiving, at Christmas, at a baptism, and soon we will be able to worship in Chalmette again. One thing that I have found that I miss the most is the strong community we had. There have been almost frantic efforts to reestablish connections, to find out where people are. And there is always rejoicing (email type) when someone is found. When I get an email from someone that has been "found," I feel a joy inside, and I realize just how much I missed them.

The harshest reality in this whole situation is that we will never have the same kinds of connections with each other that we had before. Yet we are thankful for what we have.

+ + +

The Relevance of the Church   Anton Kern

Another update from Anton Kern, dated September 27, 2005.

Hurricane Rita has increased the grief in coastal Louisiana. The western Louisiana coast looks like a less densely populated Mississippi Gulf Coast with the addition of standing water. Texas received some of the same. As hard as it is to believe, homes and businesses in Mandeville flooded again even though we were two hundred plus miles east of Hurricane Rita's center. That's the difference between being on the east side or dirty side of a hurricane rather than on the dry or west side.

In the wake of two hurricanes some things have become clear. The Church of Jesus Christ is far from irrelevant. As important as the work of the Red Cross and FEMA is to any recovery effort, I can't begin to imagine where our community would be without the churches in our community and around the country. For example, Tammany Oaks Church of Christ has become a food distribution center filling the gap created by the flooding of the Samaritan Center (our local community food bank).

Pastor Sean Ewbank did a quick count of homes and individuals receiving help from Hosanna's helping hands and estimated that seventy plus were helped in ways ranging from the removal of trees from roofs and yard to moving furniture and possessions out of flooded and condemned homes. The list of church efforts from many denominations is extensive. I can't imagine a recovery without the efforts of the Church of Jesus Christ.

Sunday we returned to our regular worship schedule of three services with 309 joining together to worship. There were many displaced persons at worship Sunday; the swollen numbers in our community are evidenced by rush hour proportioned traffic jams that exist almost all day long. I wonder what it will look like when school begins Monday.

Our schedule continues to return to normal. Next Sunday, confirmation and Sunday School will resume followed by the opening of our preschool on Monday.

We remain convinced that helping hands are the key to long term recovery. We are committed to this ministry over the long haul. Our immediate focus is restoration of the Samaritan Center and (wherever possible) homes damaged by Hurricane Katrina. We continue to believe that the sooner we reach normal in our community the sooner we can lend our hands to more severely hit communities.

+ + +

Cast Down, But Not Broken   Ron Unger

> *The following is a newsletter article from Ron Unger to the congregation of Christ the King Lutheran in Kenner, LA.*

When I asked a fellow pastor how he was doing after the hurricane, he said, "I'm cast down but not broken." He was quoting St. Paul who says, *"We are afflicted in every way, but not crushed; perplexed, but not driven to despair; persecuted, but not forsaken; struck down, but not destroyed...." (2 Corinthians 4:8-9 NRSV)*

That describes how many of us feel lately. We have undergone serious trauma and varying degrees of loss, but our spirit is not crushed and our hope not destroyed.

What a joy and relief it has been to gather again for worship after returning from the forced evacuation. How blessed we were that our sanctuary and preschool could accommodate us, and not only us but all those sisters and brothers in Christ whose churches need restoring. It was gratifying to see our members greeting each other with hugs and kisses and perhaps even more so to see folks from Grace, Gethsemane, and other congregations finding one another in our church. We have a continuing responsibility towards these fellow Christians to help them in their renewal. And we have a continuing commission from our Lord to reach out to all people with the Gospel of his love and grace.

I'm gratified to be working among you. It's been a strange transition. On September 18th I stepped before the congregation on our first Sunday back for worship and said, "I'm Ron Unger and I'm your new pastor." Although I had officially accepted your call a month earlier, I had not yet met the congregation. It was a unique way to meet. God still works in mysterious ways.

We're now serving together, "cast down, but not broken," in fact, steadily being raised to new life by our crucified yet risen Lord.

Were They to Take Our House   John McCullough Bade

The words were stuck in my throat.

I had sung the hymn on Reformation Sunday every year since I was old enough to know the words. I had been taught to stand when it was sung, even if the rubric in the bulletin indicated the congregation was to be seated. The hymn was special – the hallmark, the anthem of the Reformation: "A Mighty Fortress Is Our God."

In years past, I sang the words with gusto. Whether or not trumpets accompanied the singing, I imagined the blast of stately brass instruments leading the robustly singing congregation. But this year ... this year, as we began singing the final verse, the words stuck in my throat:

> *Were they to take our house, Goods, honor, child, or spouse,*
> *Though life be wrenched away, They cannot win the day.*
> *The Kingdom's ours forever!*

I knew there were many in church that day who had lost house, goods, and possessions. I knew there were some who had lost child, mother, father, or spouse. I knew there were some whose life as it was known was wrenched away.

And yet, they sang. They sang of a God who provides refuge and strength when all else is swept away. They sang of the sure and certain promise of life that triumphs over death. They sang of the hope of God's kingdom come at last.

Perhaps they, too, found the words stuck in their throats. Perhaps all they could utter was one word – one little word. But as the hymn proclaims, *"One little word subdues ...."* One little word gives hope and victory over all that would destroy.

"God's Word forever shall abide." A mighty fortress is our God!

Hurricane Katrina: God's Judgement?   Scott Landrum

Pastor Scott Landrum serves as pastor at Love Lutheran Church in New Orleans on the West Bank. He and his family evacuated to his mother's house in Mobile, Alabama on the Saturday prior to the storm. They had just moved into their new home ten days before the storm. The condo in which they had previously lived in Kenner flooded, but "thanks be to God our house here in Destrehan was high and dry!" (Scott's words)

Love Lutheran Church also fared very well in the storm with two member families whose homes were damaged. The church building had minor roof damage. The church has become a "refuge church" with members from four different congregations worshiping on any given Sunday.

The following is a newsletter article written by Scott in November, 2005.

I read an interesting newspaper article the other day about an Alabama state congressman sharing publicly his belief that the devastation wrought by Hurricane Katrina is God's judgement on New Orleans. With absolute confidence he proclaimed that years of unabated immorality in the "Big Easy" had finally been punished.

The man's statement is a bit odd given the fact that the epicenter of immorality, the French Quarter, remains virtually untouched by Katrina's winds. Perhaps God's aim was off if punishing immorality was the goal! I think the majority of thinking people see the ignorant lunacy of the congressman's statement and rightfully dismiss this arm-chair theologian.

On the other hand, far too many thinking people are equally confident that there is no such thing as God's judgement. One doesn't have to read far in scripture, however, to see that it is a dangerous thing to fall into the hands of an angry God. Labeling all calamity the judgement of God or denying God judges are two dangerous extremes.

So, is the catastrophe we've suffered the judgement of God or not? Before we answer that question, let us think together using a bit of Lutheran theology.

As Lutherans we teach that this world can be divided into two arenas. One is labeled those things that are above us, and the other is called those things that are below us. The things that are above us are the things that God controls apart from any input or help from us. In this arena only God has free will, not us. Our justification fits into the realm of things that are above us. God alone justifies those whom he chooses. The reasons for his choice are known only to him. Praise God he chooses you and me and gives us his promise in Word and Sacrament.

The second arena contains those things that are beneath us, the things of daily living. These include what to wear, what kind of car to drive, who to marry, where to work, etc. God has given us great latitude, "free will" to use a loaded term, in deciding our course in this arena. Not only has God granted us a tremendous amount of freedom, God has equipped us with tools for making good decisions. Among other things, God has given us the ability to reason, to be educated, and to communicate with others and share experiences. In short, God has given us everything we need to make it.

Furthermore, God expects, even demands, that we make the best decisions we can make. When we don't, we suffer the consequences. In the context of this discussion another way of thinking about consequences is passive judgement. When we disregard the tools God has given us to make it in the world below, we suffer the passive judgement of God.

Apply this to our situation here in New Orleans. We all know that this city is below sea level and should never have been settled in the first place. We all know that hurricanes have been striking this area for thousands of years. We all know that politicians both here at home and in Washington D.C. have not done enough to strengthen our hurricane protection levees or save our state from coastal erosion. We all know that we, the voters, have let them get away with it for years. We have known for years that we are extremely vulnerable to a storm.

We know all these things; and yet we choose to stay here and live. We made a decision, and part of making a decision is living with the consequences. So, yes, Hurricane Katrina is the passive judgement of God, not on immorality, but on people past and present who didn't make the best decisions possible.

Although God did not save us from the consequences of our decisions, he certainly hasn't left us to fend for ourselves either. The world has come to our aid with God-given gifts. For us personally here at Love Lutheran, our brothers and sisters in Christ from literally all over the country have partnered with us by promising to walk with us through this time of trial. They have prayed for us, volunteered to come help us rebuild and clean-up if necessary, and they have given us tremendously generous financial support.

All this goes to show that God is a gracious God who walks with us through everything.

+ + +

Comfort, O Comfort My People   Ron Unger

The following is a sermon Ron preached December 4, 2005.

"Comfort, O comfort my people, says your God."
(Isaiah 40:1 NRSV)

Oh, do we need comforting, whether we admit it or not. We were all discomforted in so many obvious ways: fleeing town, putting up with traffic jams, cramped quarters. And then we endured the results of the storm itself: power outages, ruined refrigerators, sometimes ruined homes, upset plans, scattered families, lost jobs. Oh yes, we need a whole lot of comforting; and so do all the folks around us. All of them, even the ones who look like they don't want any.

Have you had to comfort anyone lately? Foolish question. Chances are you've been doing more comforting the past few months than you have all the past few years put together. We've been comforting spouses, children, parents, neighbors, fellow parishioners, and sometimes total strangers. The list just keeps growing. And that's probably because the distress keeps mounting. Frustration grows; little is resolved. We can't bury Katrina. The aggravations crop up all over the place.

I've begun quoting Pastor Duke at Grace Lutheran, New Orleans, who has come up with the perfect comment during frustrating moments: "You mean I survived a major catastrophe just to be pestered to death by this nonsense?" I'm sure he'd let you borrow it, but it's a sign that you could use some comforting, big time.

So what's been most comforting for you? What works? Comfort food, comfortable clothing, enjoyable routines, soothing music, Bible reading, working out, family fun? Are you making enough time for it in your hectic schedule?

Don't be afraid to treat yourself kindly. You need it. And after the past couple of months, you undoubtedly also deserve it. But also be extra sensitive to the opportunity to comfort others. They need it too.

Offering comfort or trying to comfort someone in distress is one of the themes taken up in the Book of Job. Job suffers enormously; he loses everything except his life. And his wife suggests that he might as well curse God and die. She's very encouraging!

Job has three friends show up who simply sit with him in silence for seven days. That's what friends do – they show up, they're there for you, even if they don't say or do anything. It's sometimes called a ministry of presence, simply being present to another so that we're not alone in our grief.

But then Job's friends break their silence and start to try to figure out why this has happened to Job. They begin giving him unsolicited advice. It gets so bad that Job finally explodes and says, *"Miserable comforters are you all!" (Job 16:2 NRSV)*

In the book of Isaiah, the prophet is told by God, *"Comfort, O comfort my people. . . Speak tenderly to Jerusalem, and cry to her that she has served her term, that her penalty is paid, that she has received from the Lord's hand double for all her sins." (Isaiah 40:1-2 NRSV)*

God was announcing their immanent return from exile in Babylonia. The people who were taken captive would be set free, and the nation which had been destroyed would be rebuilt after eighty years of waiting. And we think we're running out of patience!

Eighty years earlier, when Jerusalem was destroyed by enemy troops, another prophet, Jeremiah, spoke his lamentation over the city. (I used portions of Lamentations for a short homily for people gathered for worship in our motel lobby in Jackson the Sunday after the hurricane.) Jeremiah begins it by saying, *"How lonely sits the city that once was full of people! How like a widow she has become, she that was great among the nations!"* *(Lamentations 1:1 NRSV)*

Later he says it this way, *"What can I say for you, to what compare you, O daughter Jerusalem? What can I liken to you, that I may comfort you, O virgin daughter of Zion? For vast as the sea is your ruin; who can heal you?"* *(Lamentations 2:13-14 NRSV)*

Yet even in the midst of this lament, Jeremiah says, *"But this I call to mind, and therefore I have hope: the steadfast love of the Lord never ceases, his mercies never come to an end; they are new every morning; great is your faithfulness. 'The Lord is my portion,' says my soul, 'therefore I will hope in him.' The Lord is good to those who wait for him, to the soul that seeks him."* *(Lamentations 3:21-25 NRSV)*

St. Paul says, *"Whatever was written in former days was written for our instruction, so that by steadfastness and by the encouragement of the scriptures we might have hope."* *(Romans 15:4 NRSV)*

So that's what I'm doing here. I'm offering the comforting words of Scripture, because even though they were originally written about another time and another place, these words come to us from the same God.

Listen to this promise, also from God to Jeremiah, *"For surely I know the plans I have for you, says the Lord, plans for your welfare and not for harm, to give you a future with hope. Then when you call upon me and come and pray to me, I will hear you. When you search for me, you will find me; if you seek me with all your heart, I will let you find me, says the Lord, and I will restore your fortunes and gather you from all the nations and all the places where I have driven you, says the Lord...."* *(Jeremiah 29:11-14 NRSV)*

Most of us feel at a loss for words when trying to comfort others. That's because there are times when only a word from God will do, like the words we've just heard. But it's even better when that word from God takes on flesh and blood, and becomes incarnate. That, of course, is what Advent is all about – waiting for the promised return of the Word made flesh in Jesus Christ. And one of the reasons we wait for him so expectantly is that he will bring the ultimate comfort.

Here's how Isaiah described his calling. The words were later used by Jesus to describe himself:

"The Spirit of the Lord God is upon me, because the Lord has anointed me; he has sent me to bring good news to the oppressed, to bind up the brokenhearted, to proclaim liberty to the captives, and release to the prisoners; to proclaim the year of the Lord's favor, and the day of vengeance of our God; to comfort all who mourn; to provide for those who mourn in Zion – to give them a garland instead of ashes, the oil of gladness instead of mourning, the mantle of praise instead of a faint spirit. They will be called oaks of righteousness, the planting of the Lord, to display his glory. They shall build up the ancient ruins, they shall raise up the former devastations; they shall repair the ruined cities ...." (Isaiah 61:1-4 NRSV)

Even so, come, Lord Jesus.

+ + +

Chapter 4
Restoration

**A Trailer in Front of a "Mucked Out" Home
A Sign of Rebuilding**

Returning Home   **Sandra Barnes**

> *Sandra reflects on the experience of returning home to Slidell, LA and gathering for the first time in worship at Christ the King Lutheran Church, Kenner, LA.*

Pastor Unger decided that we would have our first worship together on September 18, 2005, roughly three weeks after the storm. Ready or not, it was time to go home.

You would think I would be anxious to return, but leaving the relative sanctuary of my sister-in-law's house made me nervous as to what awaited us as we returned. My house was still not livable, and we were off to stay with a friend, and later with my mother-in-law who at least had some basic services – clean water and electricity.

I remember driving through Slidell, LA and seeing how things only vaguely looked the same. Hand-painted signs were all around, telling you if the water in a neighborhood was drinkable or still needed to be treated, informing you of where to find medical help, what few stores were open and what hours, where to find gas, and where MREs could be picked up. (God bless those National Guard troops for their hard work in helping pick up the pieces of our town and handling out supplies – angels in fatigues – gotta love 'em!)

It's funny; the hand-painted sign my kids were the most excited about was, "Baskin Robbins Open!" I can count on two hands and have fingers left over the number of times we actually have gone to Baskin Robbins in the roughly twenty years I have lived in Slidell, but that sign was a sign of hope for my kids – something that seemed "normal" in a world in which there was no longer "normal."

I finally went to my house, and David (my husband) met me outside. He told me not to go inside yet because it was not cleaned up enough, and he didn't believe it was safe. I looked at my front yard, which was now piled up with all of our moldy beds, furniture, carpets, clothes, toys, appliances, video tapes, photo albums, clothes, etc. (I envisioned Aladdin sitting on the top of the pile.)

While we were still in Shreveport, David had asked about starting the clean-up process, and I told him not to take "valiant measures" to save things. I thank God David was there, because I do not know if I could have just thrown out almost everything representing our almost twenty years together.

(My husband's macabre sense of humor came out gloriously at this time. When I asked him if we had lost everything, he replied, "Oh, no, the Christmas decorations are in great shape!" It turns out a few things were above the flood line.)

I sat down on a stump – the remains of a tree that came down during the hurricane – and sobbed. Funny, I only sobbed like that one other time since Katrina, which was New Year's Eve. You see, if I had been there, my instinct would have been to try to cling to some of those treasures which had so many memories.

But one of the lessons I have learned is that "things" don't hold memories; your heart does. I also felt God's presence more profoundly than at any other time in my life, which may be why I haven't really needed to fall apart more often.

I joined Pastor Unger for our first service at Christ the King Lutheran Church on September 18, 2005. You would have thought our fellowship time would never end! People stayed for hours – talking, hugging, crying joyfully. The need for the body of Christ to reconnect with each other was so incredible. Even today, after all this time, there is still a reunion of some sort every weekend as people continue to find each other and reconnect with other brothers and sisters in Christ.

Eventually, after living with other people for over two months, we received a FEMA trailer. Four people living in a thirty-foot trailer ... my son said that it was claustrophobic but a "good claustrophobic." I know what he meant; as cramped as it was, it was still ours.

We celebrated Christmas in our FEMA trailer, complete with FEMA trailer Christmas cards. I bought a tiny nativity and tree for the inside and a wreath to hang on the propane tanks. In a strange way that I can't explain other than it was truly the grace of God, we had a wonderful Christmas together.

+ + +

The Closing of a Shelter   Robin McCullough-Bade

In the days, weeks, and months after Katrina, Robin became actively involved in working with the Red Cross in communication with the local faith communities. She helped gather faith leaders in Baton Rouge for mutual support and for weekly updates from the Red Cross and FEMA. She also assisted in providing spiritual care to those in the larger Red Cross shelters in the area. One of the largest was the River Center and the adjoining Centroplex, which became shelter for thousands of people.

As FEMA trailers and other housing arrangements were secured, the shelters were no longer needed. Volunteers had poured their hearts, energies, time, and resources into the ministry offered through these places of refuge. As the River Center was closed as a shelter, Robin wrote the following liturgy which was prayed at its closing.

We gather in this place,
     to honor this building as a shelter.
We gather in this place,
     to honor those who were sheltered.
We gather in this place,
     to honor the volunteers who gave of their time.
We gather in this place,
     to honor the community and friendships formed.

This is a sacred place,
     blessed by tears and sacrifice.

Here is this place,
     people have been fed and clothed.
Here is this place,
     people have slept and found rest.

Here in this place,
>   people have received care and given care.
Here in this place,
>   children have been held and loved.
Here in this place,
>   people have told their story.

This is a sacred place,
>   blessed by tears and sacrifice.

We remember those who were sheltered;
>   we pray for peace for each of them.

We remember those who made this shelter possible
>   by giving of their time;
>   we pray for peace for each of them.
We remember those who offered their financial gifts
>   so this shelter might be made possible;
>   we pray for peace for each of them.

We remember those who continue to search
>   for what comes next after this shelter;
>   we pray for peace for each of them.

Indeed, this is a sacred place,
>   blessed by tears and sacrifice.

Go in peace,
>   knowing your acts of kindness have made a difference.

+ + +

The New Normal   **Anton Kern**

Here's another update from Anton, written October 13, 2005.

I believe the best way to describe the situation here in Mandeville and in the surrounding area is to call it "abnormally normal."

It is abnormal to have trash and debris piled up in front of your home for weeks on end. It is abnormal to have trees on roofs and sheet rock walls torn out of your home while you wait for an opportunity or contractor to replace the removed water-soaked sheet rock. It is abnormal to suddenly lose your job; and while some folks do it, it is abnormal to work in a distant city and commute home on weekends to see your family. It is abnormal to have traffic jams all day long.

What used to be abnormal has become normal.

Dr. Walt Ehrhardt spent Tuesday evening with friends and family of Hosanna Lutheran Church to help us process what we have been through. He said that we have all been traumatized – some more and some less – but none of us has escaped it. While being hit by a hurricane the size of Katrina is abnormal, to be traumatized by its effects is normal. Dr. Walt reminded us of Maslow's hierarchy of needs and said that when something of this magnitude strikes, the tendency is to regress downward rather than to move upward.

I suppose that helps to explain some of the events and actions during and following the hurricane. The traumatized responded in different ways. Some acted in violence and self-seeking, while others sought to help those who have been traumatized. While it is somewhat normal to help people in need, what is not so normal is that the traumatized are called upon to aid the traumatized. The best analogy I can think of is that the wounded have become the doctors. That's pretty abnormal.

A colleague from another part of the country asked, "How are you doing?" My answer was, "Some days pretty good, and some days not so good." Sometimes I would like to leave all the reminders of this hurricane behind for a day, but that trip is one that would take at least eight hours of driving to get away.

I've written a lot about the need for hands to help over the long haul. The people who come with their hands are the doctors. I don't think the wounded here will give up serving as doctors, but each pair of hands that comes is a little like the MASH unit getting a new doctor who is fresh for the task.

I finally was able to contact a childhood friend last week. He is living with his daughter now, and he uses his day off to restore his home which was flooded with eighteen inches of water. I told him about the groups that were coming to give us their hands. He was as blown away as we were that our brothers and sisters from the state of Washington would come and give us their hands.

When we finished our conversation he said the thought of folks coming to lend their hands had energized him.

Keep us in your prayers.

+ + +

What is Normal Now?   Sandra Barnes

Sandra continues her journal (written February, 2006) as she reflects on the "new normal" in the aftermath of the story.

I don't know if I would go so far to say things are normal; there is no longer "normal" as we have known it.

Christ the King Lutheran Church in Kenner, LA has been a staging area for Lutheran Disaster Response, and volunteer teams from around the country stay with us as they go out in loving witness and service to those still struggling and in need. We are focusing on ministries, and our children have partnered with the children of St. Paul's Lutheran Church in Ravenna, Ohio, to help support our relief efforts in the staging area. The focus is on what we can do to help the children of Katrina. The children of St. Paul's have been a delight, and working with them has been one of my personal blessings.

Personally, my own kids are in school and are involved in their various activities, which has been very therapeutic for them. I am teaching second grade. My students have this incredible need to reconnect with each other, to share their stories, to listen, and to be there for each other.

The first few days back in school were incredible, and through it all was this incredible sense of joy from everyone just to be there with one another. I experienced these same feelings as well in serving at Christ the King as an Associate in Ministry.

I am now back in my classes at Notre Dame Seminary, which may seem insane to most people, but it's typical for me! We lived out of a suitcase (more accurately, a rubber bin) for four months, but we are now "camping" in my house as we continue the rebuilding.

In spite of the magnitude of the impact of Katrina for the community as well as for me personally, I feel very blessed. The outpouring of love from friends and from brothers and sisters in Christ has just been phenomenal.

I know God has incredible plans for us, and I am ready to answer God's call in these emerging ministries before us!

"For surely I know the plans I have for you, says the Lord, plans for your welfare and not for harm, to give you a future with hope." (Jeremiah 29:11 NRSV)

+ + +

God Doing a New Thing   **Ron Unger**

A sermon by Ron, preached Feb 19, 2006 at Christ the King Lutheran Church in Kenner, LA.

"Do not remember the former things, or consider the things of old. I am about to do a new thing; now it springs forth, do you not perceive it?" (Isaiah 43:18-19 NRSV)

"A new thing." Hmm. I don't know if I can take any more new things.

We just bought a new house with all new furniture in a new community. We're in a new church and my wife has a new job. We're both wearing all new clothing. Somebody described it like living in the witness protection program. Now we're shopping for a new car because one of ours was totaled two weeks ago.

At this point I'd settle for a few old things. The new, after all, often comes at the expense of the old, and most of us are creatures of habit. We prefer the old and familiar.

This is true even in our relationship with God. Pastor Dan Duke from Grace Lutheran Church (in New Orleans) and I have been asked to be on a team of folks from our synod who will introduce a new hymnal and other worship resources in the fall. Well, I was on a similar team to introduce the green *Lutheran Book of Worship* when it was new in 1978, and it did not go smoothly. People don't take well to new worship materials. I get flack whenever I select an unfamiliar hymn even if it's been around for a few hundred years.

But God wasn't talking about worship practices when God told the Israelites, "I am about to do a new thing." No, God was about to gather up the exiles whose city and country had been destroyed about seventy years earlier, gather them up, and bring them back to rebuild.

During the evacuation, on that first Sunday after the hurricane, I led worship for about three dozen evacuees in the motel lobby in Jackson, MS. And one of the readings was from the Book of Lamentations in which Jeremiah weeps over the destruction of Jerusalem. It's powerful stuff.

Lamentations begins with this description of Jerusalem: *"How lonely sits the city that once was full of people! How like a widow she has become, she that was great among the nations! She that was a princess among the cities has become a vassal." (Lamentations 1:1 NRSV)*

But in today's First Lesson, the prophet Isaiah is assuring the people that God will be with them in their rebuilding; but there will be some changes – some predictable, others not.

First, there were the cosmetic changes. The footprint of the city and nation would be different. Jerusalem's walls were breached, so new ones would be built. The temple was so utterly destroyed that not one stone still stood upon another. It would have to be redone. And a lot of the former residents, in fact a majority of the former residents (10 out of 12 tribes) weren't ever coming back.

But those were just the obvious differences – the superficial changes. The real newness was this: that people would stop thinking of their lives only in economical, social or even political terms and start seeing themselves in relationship to God, their Creator. In the old Jerusalem the people were so wrapped up in themselves that they paid little regard to their neighbors and their fellow citizens. In fact, the only interest they had in each other seemed to be economical; i.e., how they could make more money off their fellow townspeople. It had been a really sad and superficial way to live. It had led to lots of injustice and plenty of inequities.

So the new which God was presenting to them wasn't just the opportunity to rebuild a city but a whole new social fabric or network, a community in which people would be called upon anew to *"... do justice, love kindness, and walk humbly with your God." (Micah 6:8 NRSV)*

Because that's the real issue, isn't it? Not where we're going to live, but how. Not whether we can reclaim any of our possessions, but whether our spirits will be rekindled. Not who our new neighbors will be, but whether we will be good neighbors to them. The question isn't finally whether life will go on, but what kind of life will it be?

These are the big issues, aren't they? While many of us are weighed down with a million and one questions and concerns, decisions and choices to be made, we shouldn't avoid the underlying issue, which is the question about what God may be up to in our lives, what new thing God has in mind for us.

We've heard it so often that we're finally coming to believe that New Orleans will never be the same city it once was, for better or for worse. And we've all got some role to play in its refashioning, which is exciting work as we all do our part in the rebuilding effort, both physically and spiritually, I'd hope.

But chances are we won't ever be quite the same people we were either. There's an opportunity for refashioning, reshaping and reforming here.

So what's the new thing God is doing with you?

Every day now, driving home, I pass Crossroads Church on Loyola Avenue. Since September I think they've had the same sign up in front of their church. It's a quote from Revelation, the last book of the Bible. The quote is Revelation 21:5 (NRSV): *"See, I am making all things new."*

Here are the verses leading up to it:

"Then I saw a new heaven and a new earth; for the first heaven and the first earth had passed away, and the sea was no more. And I saw the holy city, the new Jerusalem, coming down out of heaven from God, prepared as a bride adorned for her husband. And I heard a loud voice from the throne saying, 'See, the home of God is among mortals. He will dwell with them as their God; they will be his peoples, and God himself will be with them; he will wipe away every tear from their eyes. Death will be no more; mourning and crying and pain will be no more, for the first things have passed away.' And the one who was seated upon the throne said, 'See, I am making all things new.'" (Revelation 21:1-5 NRSV)

God is always way ahead of us, calling us into the future God intends for us, making all things new. And it is Christ who has gone before us, through death to resurrection, to make that the pattern of our lives too, as he calls us always out of the past and into the new of his own design.

+ + +

Encouragement   Amy Ziettlow

Pastor Amy Ziettlow is an ELCA pastor serving in the Hospice ministry in Baton Rouge. Her ministry and insight in dealing with loss has been significant and important in the aftermath of the storm. Amy's husband Michael is a pastor serving at First Christian Church in Baton Rouge, LA. This congregation opened their doors as a shelter and had evacuees living there for several months.

Amy offers a sermon preached September 19, 2005 at the Lutheran Church of Our Saviour in Baton Rouge, LA.

Times of crisis and anxiety demand response. These past few weeks have been a time of crisis and anxiety for us as individuals and families as well as for our entire community.

We have seen many responses. We have listened to our political leaders speaking of what is being done and what can be expected in the future. We have listened to our business leaders speaking of the loss of jobs, of the transfers of businesses and jobs out the area, of companies going bankrupt. We have listened to our educational leaders seeking school supplies and space for the countless new students to our areas.

We have listened to the voices of people from all over the country offering prayers for the entire Gulf Coast area as well as sending basic goods and offering hands-on help in what ever way is needed. We have listened to the voices of the countless people speaking of need, despair, and shock as they have been displaced and are looking for a home when houses are gone. We have listened to the responses of our own community, many sheltering relatives and friends, some continuing to clean up debris here and in surrounding areas, and all worrying about how we will adjust and adequately respond to all the changes in our community.

A disaster like Hurricane Katrina and its aftermath forces communities to respond on a number of levels: practical, physical, mental, political, economic, emotional, and spiritual. Both the initial event and the flurry of responses and directions of action can be confusing and almost debilitating.

I know that these past few weeks as I've gone to worship and been in prayer, I've been seeking two things: *encouragement and guidance*. I find myself wanting to know that everything is going to be okay and then wanting to know what to do – what the way forward should be.

Thankfully, scripture is full of many different people facing difficult times – times of confusion and anxiety – and yet finding encouragement and guidance from God and from each other in the midst of those times. I was especially drawn to Paul's letter to the Philippians. Not just in this letter but in almost all of his letters, Paul plays the role of both cheerleader and coach to these early church communities.

He often writes words of encouragement and guidance to these new Christian communities. Each community is facing their own struggles and difficulties, and he writes to cheer them on and to help them form a plan and vision for the future.

Paul's role as cheerleader and coach comes through clearly in the letter to the Philippians. As a cheerleader, he encourages them to remember *who they are* – to remember that they are Christians, claimed by God, accompanied by God, loved by God. He echoes words of encouragement that he writes in the letter to the Romans and reminds them that nothing can separate them from the love of God – no height, on depth, no power on earth or heaven, no hurricane, no loss of anything, can separate us from the love God; that whether we live or whether we die we are the Lord's. *(Romans 8:31-39)*

As Paul writes these words of encouragement to a struggling community, he writes to himself as well. The Philippians know that Paul is not in an easy place either. He is writing to them from jail where he is being unjustly held, persecuted for being a Christian and for publicly preaching the Gospel. He rests assured that his present predicament and place of struggle is not a reflection of who he truly is. And remembering who he is – a person of faith, claimed by God – gives him both comfort and encouragement. It helps give him guidance for how to proceed in the future.

He tells the church at Philippi of how he is preaching to the people and the guards in jail with him, how he continues to correspond with churches, and how he realizes that his purpose comes both from his relationship to Christ and his relationship to the people in the church. He recognizes that he can still be a cheerleader and coach to them from jail through his letters and through those who come to visit him. He begins to see jail as an unexpected opportunity to serve God and others.

What I appreciate about Paul's method of giving encouragement is that he doesn't expect them to make the same choices or to make the same interpretations that he does. He doesn't expect them to be a Paul clone. He wants them to know that they can find strength and encouragement from their faith, from remembering that they too are claimed and loved by God, just as he does. He points out how faith in Christ can give us a perspective different than the perspective of our own situation, and that faithful perspective can bring us both encouragement as well as wisdom and vision for where God is calling us in the future.

In terms of guidance, Paul coaches the Philippians to be of one mind – the mind of Christ. He uses the phrase: "mind of Christ" an overabundance of times in such a short four-chapter letter. He says: *"Be of one mind, be one in the mind of Christ"* in chapters one, two, three and four.

Being of one mind must be pretty important as well as pretty powerful for Paul to say it so many times. However, it must also be pretty difficult to embody to say so many times.

As the mom of a toddler, if you want to know what my son is struggling with, simply ask me what phrases or commands I repeat most often: "Don't hit you baby sister, don't say potty words, wash your hands, potty words are not funny..."

Paul repeatedly coaches the Philippians to be of one mind, the mind of Christ, not only because there is power in faithful unity, but also because being of one mind is not easy. He returns to words of encouragement, stressing that we can be of one mind, the mind of Christ, simply because we are Christ's.

Christ is the one thing we have in common, and a relationship with Christ is the one thing we have to offer. Our common bond in faith will give us guidance to know what we can offer each other – to those who are displaced, homeless and anxious, and to our community.

During these times of great change and anxiety in our community, as we seek our own encouragement and guidance, let us hear these words of Paul from chapter 2 of Philippians: *"If then there is any encouragement in Christ, any consolation from love, any sharing in the Spirit, any compassion and sympathy, make my joy complete: be of the same mind, having the same love, being in full accord and of one mind .... Let the same mind be in you that was in Christ Jesus ...."* (Philippians 2:1-2, 5 NRSV)

Amen

+ + +

Grace Upon Grace   Robin McCullough-Bade

Robin recalls a unique gift given for the recovery efforts.

Phone calls, emails, and offers to assist came unceasingly during the craziness of those first weeks. People from throughout our country and the world deeply desired to "do something" to help. Cardboard boxes packed with quilts, toothbrushes, and beanie babies showed up on the church porch unannounced.

One caller from Minnesota left several messages. His congregation wanted to donate a recreational vehicle. When we finally had a chance to talk by phone, he asked, "Could you use an RV?" I replied, "Absolutely." So many people lost their homes; I was confident an RV would be a tremendous help to some family.

A week or so passed; he called again. He had a thought: if he was coming from Minnesota, why not fill the vehicle with things we needed? Quickly, we created a list: snow shovels to muck homes, cleaning supplies, pillows, towels, empty gas containers, and many other items.

I forgot about the RVs and moved on to other matters. Days passed in a blur of activity as we tried to respond to the depths of needs. But then one day there were several more messages from Minnesota, "What if the congregation sent two recreational vehicles? What if one was brand-new? Could you find two families to use them?" "Most definitely! "

Plans were finalized. The Minnesota team with two RVs arrived Saturday, September 24, 2005, just hours before Hurricane Rita was scheduled to hit Louisiana. But they didn't just bring RVs. Every cupboard was packed to capacity with items from our "needs" list. Before leaving Minnesota, they had parked the vehicles in front of their church building and invited people to bring supplies from the list. Strangers stopped by to contribute goodwill offerings.

Amazing!

Yet due to the approach of Hurricane Rita, these ambassadors of love could not stay long and chat. Quickly, we went into the sanctuary for picture-taking and the signing over of the titles for the vehicles. Perhaps they stayed on our church property forty-five minutes before grabbing a quick Cajun lunch and then heading back to Minnesota.

Those two RVs, overflowing with gifts, were quite a sight in the parking lot. But what really touched me were the items in front of the campers. Carefully placed in a straight line were at least seven gas containers, not empty, but filled with gas – gold in those chaotic days. Gas was outrageously expensive and hard to find. Many gas stations were open only limited hours; yet these brothers and sisters of the family of Christ found the means and the time to purchase gas to fill each container.

That gift was given in addition to the bounty of RVs and their contents. It was no less than grace upon grace! Indeed, grace upon grace!

+ + +

Psalm 23

Ron Unger

Ron offers a poignant sermon based on Psalm 23, preached October 9, 2005 at Christ the King Lutheran Church, Kenner.

Today's psalm couldn't have come at a better time! It's a strong statement of faith in the midst of doubt, an expression of trust even when things are pretty gloomy, an assertion of hope though there's lots of cause for despair, and a song of gratitude in the face of tremendous loss.

It couldn't have come at a better time. We need the reminder, the example, the promise, and the comfort of this psalm. Let's meditate upon it together in the wake of Hurricane Katrina. I'll use the old, more familiar version.

"The Lord is my shepherd, I shall not want."
This may be the most difficult and challenging verse of the entire psalm, and it comes right at the beginning. There is so much we want! Some of us want our jobs back, our power restored, or our children home. We want our homes in working order again. We want to hear from our insurance adjusters. But most of all, we want our lives back the way they were – familiar, comfortable, predictable – instead of this uncertainty, confusion and worry. Many of us have a list of wants a mile long.

And yet there is a statement of faith, a statement of fact which comes even before this strange assertion, *"I shall not want."* It is the reminder, *"The Lord is my shepherd."*

We've often had the mistaken impression during this whole ordeal that we've been left to our own devices, that if we're not assertive enough or aggressive enough with FEMA, or our insurance companies, or the Red Cross, or our credit card companies, or – well, you name it – we'll be overlooked or left out. We feel it's all up to us. So we begin with the reminder that the Lord is leading us, the Lord is watching over us, the Lord is looking after our best interests, the Lord is our shepherd. And we shall not be in want.

We may not have any electricity yet, but we have God's power. We may not be sleeping in our own beds, but *"he makes me lie down in green pastures."* We may have had a surge of water crashing through our homes, but *"he leads me beside still waters, "* cleansing, purifying, clear and satisfying waters which are welcomed as a gift after those other waters which were so foul and destructive.

"He restoreth my soul."
Oh, my! Cars can be replaced; most homes can be rebuilt. As we've all said, "Those are only things." But what would it take to restore a soul? Here's the thing: we can see most mold; we can feel the dampness in carpets and sheet rock. And we know what to do to rectify those problems. But we can't see the condition of our souls. We're often unaware of how spiritually toxic our environment is, and the job of this kind of restoration is way beyond our skills and ability.

So here's the Good News: *"He restoreth my soul."* I don't. I can't. I wouldn't even know where to begin. I'd get it all wrong. Besides, it would be an endless task; I'd never finish. It would take forever and then some. I am so glad, therefore, that *"he restoreth my soul."*

"He leadeth me in the paths of righteousness for his name's sake."
Quite a few of us have felt the Lord's guidance over the past five weeks. He led us to safety, to new friends and blessed circumstances. He led us out of harm's way onto the path of life. And he hasn't stopped leading us. He continues to guide us, and we need to keep letting him guide us.

"Yea though I walk through the valley of the shadow of death, I will fear no evil."

A German Lutheran Bishop named Hans Lilje was put in a Nazi jail during the second World War because of his outspoken opposition to Hitler. While there he wrote a long meditation upon the 23rd Psalm and his experience in prison. He titled it, <u>In the Valley of the Shadow of Death</u>. He came to a profound understanding of ultimate trust in the Lord despite current circumstances.

You didn't have to be in the Superdome or Convention Center to be afraid. There's been plenty of reason for all of us to be frightened. Yet, we say with the psalmist, *"though I walk through the valley of the shadow of death, I will fear no evil."* Why? Because it's not evil? Oh, but it is.

No. *"I will fear no evil for thou art with me; thy rod and thy staff they comfort me."* You give me constant glimpses and reminders of your presence with me even in the thick of things. You are with me. Not just ahead of me, or behind me, or above me, but right along side of me.

By the way, did you notice the subtle change here from third person to second person (as my wife the English teacher would describe it)? The Lord is no longer "he" or "him," but "thou" – the extra familiar form of "you."

"Thou preparest a table before me in the presence of mine enemies."
There seems to be some gloating in this notion about being given the royal treatment right in front of those who would just as soon see us ignored or mistreated. But of course that's exactly how we are treated because of Christ. He makes us his guests of honor.

I don't know which you've experienced more of the past several weeks: mistreatment or the royal treatment. A family of strangers invited a whole bunch of us from our motel to their home for a Labor Day party. It was our first time to be in a real house eating home-cooked food since the evacuation. We were treated wonderfully.

But that's only a foretaste of the feast to come. Here also, at this table, the Lord invites us regularly to the meal he's prepared before us. It's his supper. He is the host, and we are the guests of honor all the time.

"Thou anointest my head with oil, my cup runneth over."
That's just another way of describing the Lord's lavish grace.

We are all now survivors of the greatest natural disaster to ever occur in the United States. Whenever we tell someone over the phone that we're from New Orleans, they immediately say, "Oh, I'm so sorry." We've been marked as "those poor people." We're afraid that's how we'll always be regarded.

But we see ourselves differently. Because of God's grace, mercy and love, we can say confidently, *"Surely goodness and mercy shall follow me all the days of my life."* Don't feel sorry for us. God is with us. The Lord is our shepherd. Goodness and mercy shall follow us all the days of our lives, and we *"will dwell in the house of the Lord forever."*

The Lord's house – high and dry and full of life and joy.

+ + +

A Strange Kind of Math   Anton Kern

Another update from Anton, Hosanna Lutheran Church, Mandeville, LA, dated October 26, 2005.

Hi friends,

Progress is slow. The enormity of the task of putting things back together creates a wave of emotions from discouragement to hopefulness. The task is a lot like eating an elephant one bite at a time. The first bites go down easy, but after a while there is a sense of fullness that makes each succeeding bite more difficult. A friend mine reminds me that you have to focus on one small part and get a victory. Then you can move on to another bite.

There is frustration, too. It has been said that information is power. The lack of information as to what insurance settlements will be creates a great deal of frustration and inhibits progress and forward movement. Until my insurance adjuster comes by with an estimate, the roof remains patched and the fence remains down. Without that information I can't make a decision concerning the what, when and how of repairs.

So I wait.

It's even worst for small businesses as they wait for a decision on gap insurance settlements. (That's the insurance they carry on interruption of business.) And they wait for claim adjustments on flood insurance, wind damage and contents. Until they have that information it is difficult to make a sound business decision.

There are signs of improvement, too. How wonderful it was to have the eight-feet-high by four-feet-wide by fifty-feet-long pile of debris removed from my front lawn. The logs and the limbs are slowly being removed from our neighborhood. East of Mandeville one span of the Interstate I-10 bridge from Slidell to New Orleans has reopened. Traffic seems a little lighter in Mandeville, but it is far from its pre-Katrina days.

There are ministry opportunities, too. A newspaper article this week indicated that the estimated population of St. Tammany Parish (a parish in Louisiana is the equivalent of a county everywhere else) was 217,000 at the end of 2004. The estimate now stands at 300,000. That's 83,000 people in search of healing, a new church home, or some answers to the meaning of life in the face of this catastrophe. We are struggling to rise to meet those ministry opportunities.

It's hard to describe the experience here. We spend a lot of time trying to convince ourselves that we really don't have any problems when compared to people in St. Bernard Parish where homes were flooded for weeks, or to the folks on the Gulf Coast whose homes were leveled. And by comparison we don't.

But as Dr. Walt Ehrhardt reminded us, we have all been traumatized. Today when I met with him, he talked about the vicarious trauma experienced by those of us who have had relatively little damage. I guess I would describe it like we are all in the same ditch – some of us with flesh wounds and some of us almost mortally wounded.

As I search for words to express what we feel, I think that "alone" might be the best word to describe the feeling. It is hard to explain the feeling of aloneness with so many of us in the ditch together. It gets worst when politicians and people across the nation say it is our own fault and we don't deserve any help. The feeling moves toward feeling forsaken.

I cannot begin to express what your coming to give us your hands means and does for us. I tell each group that they are a reminder that we are not alone. They are a reminder that we are not forsaken.

There is a strange kind of synergy and solidarity that takes place. Your presence is more than the presence of a visiting dignitary who comes to survey the situation and to promise aid. It is more than the work that is accomplished. It is in a strange and mysterious thing – your presence, joined with the work, embodies Christ is with us. We are neither alone nor forsaken.

Wonderful things are happening through your helping presence. There are far too many to mention here, but there are a few I think would be good to mention. The Samaritan Center (our local interfaith food pantry and help center) had been flooded. Teams had gutted the buildings, and two weeks ago the estimates were that maybe the Center would be up and running by sometime in January.

Then your hands and hearts began to arrive. Two weeks ago some of the workers from Washington State began installing the sheet rock. Last week a group of Quakers stayed with us for the week and were determined to complete the taping, floating, and texturing to have the place paint-ready before leaving. This past weekend young adults from Concordia Lutheran College in Moorehead, MN came and painted the Center. Only the floors remain to be installed. Reopening will probably take place by mid-November.

We began with a simple vision as we sensed God's call to be a staging place for groups to come and help. We wanted to begin in our community by helping folks who couldn't help themselves, then helping those who would become helping hands, and eventually pushing out to New Orleans and the Gulf Coast.

There is a strange kind of paradox going on here as groups come to help us. We have been most thankful for their presence and help. What has continued to amaze both me and the members of Hosanna is how many times the helpers said, "Thank you for letting us come." Pastor Sean and I helped bring a group that had worked here with us for a week to the airport. As we were bidding farewells, one guy said to me, "This is the best vacation I ever had."

Both we the receivers and our guests the givers are blessed by the same gift. That is a strange kind of math – one gift and two blessings.

A friend on mine who was what I call "apprehended by grace," or "arrested by the gospel," or "mugged by God" describes things this way, "The gospel is so easy it is hard." He goes on to say that it is backwards and upside down.

And so it is, my brothers and sisters, and so it is.

Until next time....

+ + +

A New Kind of Ministry

Jim Shears

Jim reflects on the unexpected opportunity for ministry before him as Gethsemane Lutheran Church in Chalmette looks toward the future.

The most exciting prospect for me as I look to the future is the prospect of a new kind of ministry. How many pastors have the chance to start over and completely reshape a ministry in a community where they already have an established track record? And with an existing core of committed members! It's an opportunity that most never get.

At the same time, I find myself asking, "Why did God choose me for this? Can I handle this? Has God equipped me for the task?" It's an awesome and scary opportunity. I am thrilled by the prospect and awed by the responsibility. And now, I find myself impatient to get rolling. I just have to remember that it will all happen in God's time.

The last six months have been a God-experience for me. I don't believe God actively sent the hurricane, but God certainly allowed it. Hurricanes have a geological purpose, and we just got in the way.

But the hand of God has been highly visible ever since for those who can see it. God has tested and saved people, offered himself to them, gathered resources, and raised up servants as only a catastrophe can. I would love to see a dollar figure on what God's people have done compared to what the government has done. I know that God is present in all of this and has become the center of my conversations.

When everything has been taken away (in this case, except family), God always remains. It has been very easy, in light of that, to put the recovery in God's hands. I find myself looking much harder than before for the hand of God at work. It's like I expect to see it; and God hasn't disappointed me yet.

Beginnings!   **Walton Ehrhardt**

Walt concludes his reflections from September 7, 2005 with some thoughts on beginnings.

Beginnings take place in life each day.

I learned on Labor Day that we said good-bye to a wonderful pastor, teacher, theologian, and friend, a thoroughly human being and man of faith. The Rev. John Claypool died on Monday. John was our theologian-in-residence at Trinity Episcopal Church in New Orleans. The celebration of his life is in Birmingham on Friday.

He taught a very simple element of faith: *"Life is gift!"* John helped me to see that the Christian life is always about accepting what life challenges us to live, about living in the certainty that God is, and that God is in us. We experience "God" as love, an "unmerited caring," and that caring comes only through one another.

Whenever we exit from one place in life, we enter into another. It is there that new beginnings are made.

We are all making new beginnings!

+ + +

The Long Road Ahead   Anton Kern

Another update from Anton, dated December 14, 2005.

Dear Friends,

It has been a long time since I posted an update in the aftermath of Hurricane Katrina. I think it is because we have moved from a sprint-like pace of rapid change to a marathon-like pace of pressing forward one step at a time, all the while waiting for updated information that can help us make good decisions.

At the peak of the jogging craze in the late 1970s and early 1980s, one of those inspirational posters hung in the welcome area of a congregation I served in a small town in Texas. The image was of a lone jogger running up and down the steepest hills I have ever seen stretching far into the horizon beyond where the eye could see. The caption read, "The race is not always to the swiftest, but to those who keep on running."

That says it all for the area devastated by Katrina. There can be no swift recovery. If nothing else, there are still unanswered questions of what kind of levees the U.S. Corps of Engineers will build, what the new elevation requirements for rebuilding homes will be, what the end result of the insurance debate will be as to whether it was flood damage or hurricane damage, when adequate housing will be available, when all the schools will be open. The list goes on.

There are indications that some are dropping out of the race. While I have not seen published statistics, my reading of the newspaper, my conversations with health care professionals, and my own personal observations give me a sense that alcohol, drugs, and suicide are increasingly seen as a way of dropping out.

While many wonderful promises from the nation's capital have been made, the allocation of funds is moving very slowly. A recent New York Times editorial raised the question as to whether slow movement to action would cause the help promised to disappear when the next hurricane hits somewhere else in America.

I don't believe people of New Orleans expect America to fix everything; but I do know they want to know at what level of flood protection the Corps of Engineers will repair the levees, and at what elevation they will need to rebuild their homes. To ask the people of Louisiana in our area to write their congressional leaders, who are already hard at work on the problems, would be of little value. However, to ask those of you who don't live in Louisiana to write your congressional leaders would produce a much more powerful result.

There is a strange thing that happens when you live day after day and week after week with the aftermath of a hurricane. After a while things begin to look normal.

At Hosanna Lutheran Church in Mandeville, Pastor Sean and I have been living on a week-to-week basis. Our fall ministry plans had to be abandoned, and we knew it was time to do some longer range planning. To get away, we traveled to a sister congregation in Shreveport, Louisiana. As we traveled around town with a clear blue sky, the sun brightly shining, and the trees shimmering with golden leaves, we both remarked, "Wow, I didn't know Shreveport was so beautiful."

While it certainly is a pretty town, the real truth is we had become numb to our surroundings back home. In Shreveport, we were in a town where all the trees were upright, where the skyline wasn't filled with blue tarps protecting roofs from leaking, where front lawns were not covered with debris ranging from tree limbs to everything gutted from inside of homes, and where there were no massive traffic jams. We had simply come to see our own abnormal landscape as normal.

The other day I heard a story about a pastor on the New Orleans side of Lake Pontchartrain who periodically took work groups for a tour of the devastation in the New Orleans. After driving through neighborhood after neighborhood of destruction and preparing to enter the lower ninth ward, he would say to them, "Now you will see the real destruction." In disbelief they would look at him as if to say, "Well then, what were we looking at before?"

Among the many things work groups do for us when they come in to help with repair is remind us that even in our less affected part of the world, this is not normal. They remind us that we are not alone. They multiple the number of hands to help, and they speed up the recovery. They remind us that we are part of something far larger than ourselves – that we are part of the holy catholic and apostolic church that spans time and place. For this we are grateful.

Over and over, I am asked, "How can we help? What can we send?" The answer is the same: "Send us your hands and your hearts." We will need them for years to come. We are in a marathon. The race is not always to the swiftest, but to those who keep on running.

+ + +

Elevation   John McCullough Bade

In early June, 2006, several of the Lutheran faith leaders from South Louisiana were gathered in Colorado for a time of retreat, reflection and renewal. This poem was written at that retreat.

Life and death in balance held.
Sky-stretched trees uprooted, felled
         by rushing wind and surging tide.
            Lives destroyed, hope denied,
     Lost …
         but for Elevation.

Grief unmasked, wounds laid bare.
Measureless loss, pain, sorrow, despair
         waft to God in tear-filled voice –
            burdens unspoken, borne not by choice,
     Lifted up …
         by the Elevation.

Sea-leveled lives to snow-capped came
Submerged in sorrow, water-marked, stained,
         respite-longing, sanctuary-sought,
         wearied wanderers, emotions taut,
     Carried …
         to the Elevation.

Body broken, grace outpoured.
Pure-streamed cleansing, hope restored.
         Death and life in balance held;
            Nail-marked hand by love compelled –
     Incarnate …
         in the Elevation.

+ + +

A Future With Hope   **Rob Moore**

Pastor Rob Moore serves as Assistant to the Bishop in the Texas/Louisiana Gulf Coast Synod, ELCA. Rob has been instrumental in coordinating the synod's response to the hurricanes. He has been a great support for the ELCA leaders, assisting to communicate information, needs, and opportunities to help to the larger church.

The following was written by Rob for the December, 2005 edition of the synodical newsletter, The Grapevine.

As we continue to hear the stories and see the pictures of devastation coming from the areas hit by Hurricanes Katrina and Rita, it is easy to feel discouraged and overwhelmed. I feel that way as I write this article, sitting in the synod office – a place that received very little damage from the gulf coast hurricanes.

And as much as I have seen the damage and talked with those going through it, I know that I am only experiencing a fraction of what our sisters and brothers who are in the center of the affected areas are going through on a daily basis.

The recovery efforts will be a ministry that will be going on for years, even decades. This is beyond the scope of any other natural disaster to affect the United States. (For example, one report has stated that more oil was dumped into New Orleans because of the hurricanes than all the oil that was released in the Exxon Valdez oil spill.) No governmental or religious organization was prepared for destruction on such a scale. The need, as well as the response, has been overwhelming.

We are not, however, a people without hope. In the 29th chapter of Jeremiah, our Lord says to the people, *"For surely I know the plans I have for you, says the Lord, plans for your welfare and not for harm, to give you **a future with hope**." (Jeremiah 29:11 NRSV)*

Much of the hope we have received has come through people like you – people who have offered their time, talents, and financial resources for hurricane relief. You are the voice of hope, and the voice of our Lord, to our brothers and sisters in need.

Thank you for being in partnership with us as together we work to recover. It will be a long and often frustrating time, but we know that our Lord is with us every step of the way. Your voices and your gifts help to remind us that we all have a future with hope.

+ + +